N

C 2-00

MODERN SALMON FISHING

FISHING THE VOSS RIVER, NORWAY

MODERN
SALMON FISHING

BY

ANTONY BRIDGES

SECOND EDITION

WITH SEVENTEEN PLATES
AND THIRTY-FOUR LINE ILLUSTRATIONS

ADAM & CHARLES BLACK
LONDON

First published 1939
Reprinted 1947 *and* 1963
Second edition 1969

A. AND C. BLACK LIMITED
4, 5 AND 6 SOHO SQUARE LONDON W.1

SBN: 7136 0907 9

MADE IN GREAT BRITAIN
PRINTED BY R. & R. CLARK, LIMITED, EDINBURGH

INTRODUCTION TO THE
SECOND EDITION

NOBODY can be more surprised than the author at the Publishers' decision to make a fourth printing of this plain little book, which fishermen, it seems, have been buying for nearly thirty years, God bless them! I only hope they have found it worth while; and I apologise for so much uncorrected talk of "gut", when nylon has been with us for such a long time.

In this edition I have tried to take account of the new gear, mentioned in the Note to the third printing but not then included in the text. The Gut Table, which was scrapped from the Appendix in the third printing, has been reintroduced as it applies to mono-filament nylon. ("Gut", in the general text, means nylon, unless otherwise stated.) A note has also been added showing the thicknesses of tapered lines and the letters by which they are now known.

Apart from the major effects of the plastics revolu-tion, several obvious improvements have materialised —the compartmented box for salmon flies, the gaff-cum-wading-staff with a simple but adequate sling, a finger-brake for fly reels, and a power-factor for rods by which they can be suited to the required weight of line. Thanks to designers and engineers, and to the good sense of fishermen themselves, we can now fish for salmon with gear that is a delight to use.

The great remaining problem, that gets worse in-stead of better, is finding any salmon to catch.

This is critical. I touched on it in the Note to the

third printing of this book; but I ask the reader's permission to do more than that now, because I believe that unless more is done, and done quickly, "modern salmon fishing" with rod and line will very soon become a waste of time.

It is difficult to imagine what the run of salmon must have been in English and Scottish rivers when St. John wrote his "Wild Sports of the Highlands". We only know, for certain, that salmon was one of the cheapest foods available, because apprentices objected to being given so much of it, and obtained legislation whereby their indentures restricted its issue to three days a week. Now, it is worth 10/- a lb., on the bank. Rivers where it still swims, when not reserved for the entertainment of Britain's foreign customers, to help sustain the balance of payments, cost up to £10 a yard. There is no need to labour the point. In the British Isles there are a hundred times as many fishermen as in St. John's day, and not one-tenth the number of fish. The contrast is appalling, from any point of view. It is the more appalling when the numbers, the needs, and the financial emancipation of a whole new generation of rod-fishermen are seriously considered.

We need to get the fishing priorities right. In an industrial country, I believe, the first is to ensure that as many people as want to fish with a rod and line shall have the maximum chance of finding fish to catch, commensurate with what the fish cost to provide and with how many they are prepared to pay for. It costs perhaps five or ten times as much to catch a salmon on a rod as it does to net a salmon in the sea. Rod-fishing, with its attendant hotels, bailiffs, transport, etc., is a "service" industry. But it is a *holiday* industry. The £50 (or more) that so many people take abroad would be spent here if there were adequate inducement to do so. I—and perhaps a quarter of a million others—can think of no more adequate inducement than a fortnight on a Highland salmon river—if there were enough salmon in it. And the foreigner would think the same, and bring probably £100 with him, instead of taking it to Ireland or to Patagonia.

What is the trouble? And what can be done about it? The trouble, as always, is the attitude of mind that puts *immediate* financial gain at the top of any and every list of considerations. The curse of English rivers is pollution; they have been turned into sewers, through sheer indifference plus actual refusal to spend the necessary money to keep them clean. A son of mine, who flies helicopters from a base in Cornwall, has told me of the stains which spread out to sea from the mouths of our rivers in the finest summer weather. The twin curses of Scottish rivers are netting and poaching.

Largely through private initiative, a start has been made with legislation against pollution and poaching. If we can clean our streets we can clean our rivers; but *only* if public opinion is educated into wanting it done. The traditional poacher, who snags a fish for his table, does little harm to a river. The power to confiscate vehicles has begun—but only begun—to curb the organised poaching gang whose objective is not a fish to eat, but a quick couple of hundred pounds for a night's work. Legal nets at the river mouth still take far too big a proportion of fish; in many it is now over 90 per cent of the total catch. But the most recent and potentially frightful danger is offshore netting, made possible by cheap sonar.

This began, on the feeding-grounds off the west coast of Greenland, in 1965. In 1966 one boat caught 75 tons of salmon; and in 1967 ten boats were fishing there. At an average weight of 10 lb. a fish, 75 tons is 16,800 salmon. *This is more than the total yearly catch of fish, both by nets and rods, in the Wye.* It is about three times the catch on what is accounted a good small river, such as the Tavy.

Action to deal with it has to be international— through the International Commission for the North-west Atlantic Fisheries or the International Council for the Exploration of the Sea. It has been proposed that taking salmon by any means in international waters should be prohibited. This should be only the beginning. What *are* "international waters" in these days? Very heavy catches have been taken by offshore boats working drift nets near the mouth of the Tay. Salmon have coastal as well as deep-sea "routes", and these can now be discovered by echo-sounder. This business should be scotched, stone-dead, before it acquires the strength of a political lobby.

Let us face it. Salmon are going the way of the whale, unless we do something about them, and do it at once. The colour of this era, which gave us the fixed-spool reel, has also given us electronics; and, in releasing every man's greed, allows us at the same time to destroy our environment, if we are too stupid, too prejudiced, too indifferent, or too mean to preserve it.

It is time that rod-fishing, in all countries, got the consideration it deserves—shall we say, which people who want to fish are desperately in need of. What is "everybody's", without conservation or control, soon ceases to exist.

To industrial governments fisheries have always been a poor relation. Commercial sea fishing has had some hearing in the past thirty years. The attitude that rod-fishing is to be sneered at, ignored, or attacked, as a perquisite of the rich, or, at best, as an undesirable, because individual, occupation, is something that takes no account either of the number of fishermen today or of what fishing means to them. Any man who does his job in an industrial town, and is allowed out only for a fortnight in the year, ought to have the best that his money can buy. Too few people in authority either understand the national economic worth of licensed rod-fishing of decent quality, or appreciate in the smallest degree the human needs and benefits involved. It is time our vaunted "education for leisure" took account of leisure's more wholesome forms. "Conurbation" leaves us few enough of them.

There are, of course, too many fishermen for too little water, and it is difficult to estimate what could be offered to each. A comparison with Ireland is invidious, because in Ireland there is much water, and, although every third man is a fishermen, there are still few enough men; and, as yet, little industrial and urban filth. However (to illustrate what still happens), the mill hands at Foxford, on the Moy, averaged in 1967 about 40 salmon apiece, at a cost of £1. 10. 0 for a State licence and £1 a year for the Club water, which has been cheaply leased to them by its owner. Ireland, of course, is fast filling up with fishermen in holiday-time; but the State-subsidised Fishery Trust does an immense amount to conserve and improve the rod-fisheries, and the government itself recognises and respects them as a national asset.

Whatever test is applied to salmon-fishing in an overcrowded industrial country, the rod-fisherman will be found to represent "the greatest good of the greatest number". In our evolutionary—or revolutionary—zeal, we are apt to forget that the "collective" is composed of individuals, upon whose separate health it depends.

AUTHOR'S NOTE
TO THE THIRD PRINTING

THE twenty years that have passed since this book was first published have seen changes, social and technical, as great as any in history, and the sport of salmon fishing has not escaped their effects. The gear now available is more efficient and—amazingly, in view of what has happened to the value of money—much cheaper. The finely split sections of specially selected cane that went to make the best rods have now given place to the hollow fibreglass tube made by lapping woven glass cloth on a mandrel and setting it with resin. There is practically no difference in the resulting action. Those brought up with split cane, as I was, may contend that it still has more stiffness, more fire, for the same weight; but I am afraid we should be arguing less from fact than from ancient prejudice and affection. The fibreglass rod is good, and it is cheap. It weighs no more. It can be reproduced exactly, in any action, and to throw anything, from a heavy spinner to a dry fly.

We have also said good-bye to the blued, tapered, and expensive cast that was made up from short lengths of silkworm gut. Gut has gone for good; and we need shed no tears over that, since nylon, extruded by the mile in sizes accurate to the ten-thousandth of an inch, and very cheap, is in every way a better article. It is stronger and clearer; it needs no soaking; it does not crack. It is more slippery and needs secure knotting; but most of the gut knots will serve, and the same principles apply. To sink a nylon cast for greased-line fishing, rub it over with fuller's earth: grease slipping down the line then does not matter.

For fly-fishing we still use the same reels, but now the line is coated with plastic, so there is an end of sticky dressings. For spinning, the fixed-spool reel—developed in every size and grade from the old Illingworth pattern—is universal; and there is no longer any separation between line and trace, but only a spool of nylon, the size of which is measured by its breaking strain and can be suited exactly to the business in hand.

The reverse side of the post-war revolution is seen in the dwindling stock of salmon. There is more money, cheaper and better gear: hence more fishermen; and that, in itself, is good. But there are fewer and fewer fish to go round. The cost of a good beat is now so high that the tendency—often the necessity—is to pay for it in fish caught: so that the sport becomes half business. Netting, pollution, and hydro-electric schemes add to the toll. The remedy is conservation, and co-operation to the point where any man, at reasonable cost, has a good chance of catching a fish or two during his holiday. Such an end is surely worth pursuing, not only by fishermen, but by all in this crowded age who understand the value, in terms of human sanity, of a great outdoor sport.

A. B.

1962

TO

Lieutenant R. H. CONNELL, R.N.

Though the crew we knew are fledged and flown,
  They say The Ship still stands;
That the cod still come to the Anchor Stone
  And the bass to Slapton Sands;
While up the Dart past Dittisham
  The salmon swim from sea
To hang in the pools by Hexworthy
  For the likes o' you and me!

The Fates have flung our paths apart,
  While the wheeling seasons wait:
You the Outer Seas to chart,
  I to sit in the Gate.
But the kindly seasons wait
  To return us to Earth again—
To the smell of the bog myrtle
  And the river's roar in the rain.

PREFACE

Any general book on salmon fishing must suffer from two particular limitations.

In the first place, there are exceptions to practically every statement that can be made on the subject. Every generalisation is simply a desperate attempt to see in one set of experiences some grain more virtue than appears to be contained in a set of equal and opposite ones. Throughout the book I have given as fully as possible the reasons for any stated conclusion, but the reader would be wise to accept these as no more than a working basis. His own experiences may lead him to think very differently.

Secondly, salmon fishing is both a science and an art. A science can be set out in so many words and learnt; an art can only be hinted at. Its interpretation may take a hundred forms, and the excellence lies not in the form but in the interpreter. One may say that to cast a fly the arms should be moved thus, and that to fish a pool one proceeds in this way or that way, but the fact is, one may follow written instructions to the letter and not become a fisherman. The artistry of fishing is a thing that grows, moulded by the thousand unheeded influences of long days beside the river, till a man catches fish without knowing why he does so. No fisherman, thank Heaven, ever learnt his craft out of a book. There is no last word. Each initiate steps anew into a clear morning and has his own long day in front of him.

Within these limits, then, I hope the book may be found helpful and not without interest.

It is very pleasant to be able to thank the kindly people who have helped me make it. To the Norwegian National Tourist Office I owe the photographs by Mr Arthur Oglesby of the Voss River in the frontispiece and of Bardufoss (facing page 102), and to Mr James Mackintosh, of the Canadian Pacific Railway, that on page 206. Mr Finn de Lange was kind enough to send me from Bergen the picture on page 199 (bottom left). Mr Courtney Williams, of Messrs Alcock & Co., wrote to me about hook scales and Mr Jack Lyons, of Cork, about the weights and construction of rods. To Mr W. J. M. Menzies and to Mr John Rennie, of the Perth Museum, I am indebted for help and advice, as I am to Mr Cummins and Colonel Pearson. Mr Arthur Hutton very generously sent me the photographs which appear on pages 22, 30, 103, 174, 175, 198, and two of those on page 199. Finally it is with a deep sense of gratitude that I say, "Thank you" to my friend Mr H. D. Turing, who, by his constant kindness and encouragement, has made my writing of this book not only a possibility but a delight.

A. B.

INNER TEMPLE
March 1939

xvi

CONTENTS

CHAP.   PAGE

Chapter	Title	Page
I.	UNTO THE HILLS	1
II.	THE SALMON FISHERMAN'S DEAD RECKONING	6
III.	FIXED ASSETS	23
IV.	THE DELICATE ART OF WADING	35
V.	SUNK FLY—GEAR	45
VI.	THE MECHANICS OF FLY-CASTING	69
VII.	SUNK FLY—ORTHODOX AND HETERODOX	81
VIII.	FROM A VIEW TO A DEATH	96
IX.	PACKING AND COOKING SALMON	108
X.	GREASED LINE—IDEAS AND OUTFIT	114
XI.	FISHING THE GREASED LINE	126
XII.	"DAPPING"	135
XIII.	DRY FLY	142
XIV.	SPINNING GEAR	148
XV.	SPINNING IN HEAVY WATER	166
XVI.	SPINNING IN LOW WATER	172
XVII.	ROVING A PRAWN	178
XVIII.	WORMING	188
XIX.	SALMON IN LAKES	195
XX.	BIOGRAPHY	202
XXI.	HOW A RIVER CAN BE IMPROVED	207
APPENDIX:	A SALMON FISHERMAN'S TABLES	217
INDEX		219

2   xvii

ILLUSTRATIONS

PRINTED SEPARATELY FROM THE TEXT

FISHING THE VOSS RIVER, NORWAY . . . *Frontispiece*

FACING PAGE

"BETWEEN LOWLAND AND HIGHLAND" . . . 22

A POOL ON THE TUMMEL BELOW GUAY . . . 23

A CLEAN SALMON AND A PROPER GAFF⎱
ALMOST A KELT ⎰ . . . 30

A SQUARE CAST ON THE WARREN 31

A 25-POUNDER FROM BARDUFOSS . . . 102

WALKING A FISH IN TO THE GAFF . . . 103

THE FAMOUS DIRT-POT POOL ON THE TWEED AT CARDRONA 110

CONVENIENT POSITIONS WHEN CASTING WITH THE AERIAL
AND THE PFLUEGER 111

THE ALTEX STATIONARY-DRUM REEL . . . 166

WHERE A BOAT IS A NECESSITY 167

A 20-LB. COCK FISH IN FULL SPAWNING LIVERY ⎱
A 22-LB. HEN FISH WHICH HAD SPAWNED BEFORE⎰ . 174

SOME LITTLE ONES 175

CLUES TO THE PAST 198

SOME BIG ONES 199

SALMON ASCENDING THE FRASER RIVER, B.C. . . 206

OUR FRIENDS FROM THE TIDEWAY 207

PRINTED IN THE TEXT

PAGE

DIAGRAM TO SHOW THE DEDUCTIONS FROM A ROCK BOIL 13

LIGHT BEHIND THE BAIT 19

PAGE

LIGHT IN FRONT OF THE BAIT 19

THE WHIP FINISH 27

GAFF AND SLING 28

TAILPIECE 34

SHOWING HOW A WHALEBACK IS FORMED BY FLOODS . 38

BLOOD KNOT: WRONG WAY 51

BLOOD KNOT: RIGHT WAY 51

THE BLOOD KNOT DRAWN TIGHT 52

DOUBLE FISHERMAN 52

SIMPLE OVERHAND LOOP KNOT 53

BLOOD LOOP 53

DOUBLE CAIRNTON 54

SINGLE CAIRNTON 54

TURLE KNOT 55

SHEET BEND 55

GUT THICK ENOUGH 57

GUT TOO THIN 57

OVERHEAD CAST 70

SWITCH CAST 74

SPEY CAST 75

THE EFFECT OF A SQUARE CAST ACROSS FAST WATER . 78

THE EFFECT OF MENDING A SQUARE CAST . . 79

MENDING 80

THE TRAVELLER 90

RETRIEVING A CAST 91

TAILPIECE 147

PRAWN MOUNTED ON A TWEED TACKLE . . . 154

THE TWEED TACKLE 154

BAYONET PRAWN TACKLE 183

SINGLE HOOK, BAITED 192

TWO-HOOK WORM TACKLE 192

ROD TABLE 218

xx

MODERN SALMON FISHING

CHAPTER I

UNTO THE HILLS

Salmon fishing is the greatest of all the sports, that can be had in fresh water. . . . The attraction of it is found in the largeness of the fish, the size of the rivers, the strength of the stream, and the tremendous uncertainty.

VISCOUNT GREY OF FALLODON, *Fly Fishing*

IN salmon fishing, as in most other recreations, there is seen to be increasing that homely and derided virtue, common sense. It is a phenomenon of recent growth, due to the habit of concentrated thought which seems necessary in these days for the very business of keeping alive. We no longer cycle on "penny-farthings", play cricket in top hats, nor sail round the world on bar-relled beef and weevily biscuits. The salmon fisherman used to thrash the long day through with a 20-foot rod and a rickety pirn, but he does so no longer. He is using modern engineering knowledge to knock off these ancient shackles and free himself for the finer problems.

One can never improve an art too much. Probably, when dictators cease from troubling and it becomes *démodé* to hunt in a polished saddle, life will no longer be worth living. But these things are out of sight, and in the meantime inventions like plastic lines and the stationary-drum reel have increased rather than less-ened the salmon fisherman's enjoyment of his craft.

There is nothing miraculous, nor even subversive, in these inventions. They do not abolish all problems. They merely make it possible to tackle fresh ones, of a nicer texture. They are simply mechanical improvements, like the hot-plate cooker or the Bermudan sail, which replace much of what was dull by much of what is interesting.

The reason behind these innovations is that salmon fishermen have arrived at ideas which demand a departure from the old-fashioned tackle and methods. It is seen nowadays that fishing tackle must be in proportion, and that its size has very little to do with the size of the fish, but depends chiefly on the size of the fly or bait used. It must be fine, too, for a salmon is not a wild beast, to be attacked, but a timid creature, to be stalked. Fineness in gear is not only pleasant and necessary ; it is also *possible*. A 15-foot rod, for instance, bent until the tip makes 90 degrees with the butt, will not break OX gut, and a salmon, it has at last been realised, is too powerful a creature to be hauled out by force, but can easily be worried, even with the finest gear, into exhausting itself.

It is generally agreed, too, that spinning does not necessarily spoil a pool for the next man, but that if a fly fisherman objects it is polite to humour him; that it is courteous to give the methods of local inhabitants a chance—for so long as they continue to catch fish; that it is easier to be careless, but that it spoils one's fun; and that what was good enough for our grandfathers is not invariably good enough for us.

It seems, too, that there is a boom in that ultimate wisdom which fishermen and other "honest men" have possessed since the race began—the leaving for a space the toil and hurry of crowded places, and finding peace once more in the wild. Diocletian found it beside the trout streams of Dalmatia, and it came to the Psalmist when he lifted his eyes to the hills. It is a prescription which many of us need, and which more and more of us are wise enough to take. I think that the chief joy of fishing is that it is both single-handed and uncompetitive. The pleasure of the salmon fisherman is like that of the lone yachtsman or the mountaineer, rather than like that of the fox-hunter or the shooting man. The salmon fisherman is generally alone, but he is always occupied; his object does not press urgently upon him, yet it is sufficiently primitive to keep him alert and expectant; and his day is spent in clean air, amid the comfortable roar of the river—a voice that lies easily upon the senses and requires no answering.

The essence of salmon fishing is hugeness of water and surroundings. Trout fishing can be pretty and idyllic. Salmon fishing is always—to use an abused word in the sense that a Scottish gillie uses it—grand.

The salmon fisherman moves less far than the moorland trout fisherman; he is not quite such a highlander. But his game is, if he cares to make it so, more exacting. To climb in waders down a cliff in order to reach a ledge to cast from, with twenty feet of black, rocking water beneath, to edge inch by inch across a fast current, or to be compelled to pursue a fish, in a steep river like the Dart, by following, from rock to rock, a course which in cold blood would make an Alpine climber hesitate—these things demand nerve and physical fitness of a high order. Salmon fishing can be what the fisherman cares to make it. Where a boat is used— and a boat in the broad lower reaches of many rivers is a necessity—it can be a quiet and peaceful recreation. For a strong man on a rough river it can compare, for sheer stress and excitement, with any sport in the world.

3

The salmon fisherman sees as much as the trout fisherman of birds and beasts. Parts of many rivers are lovelier and more populous than any garden. The great buttresses of forest in the valleys of the lower Eden, the Tamar, the Teign, or the Double Dart, for instance, contain innumerable wild creatures, and the fisherman, because he is busy at his own affairs, stumbles on them, at theirs, more often than he ever would if he had set out to look for them. On the high moor, too, "at the back of beyond", on a river like the upper Findhorn, there are reminders of a sterner wild. There the wandering fisherman may hear the persistent croak of a raven about the black towers of some mountain face, and see the distant slow-swinging dot which is a peregrine or an eagle. A sudden swish of wings round a brae-head and an explosive "cock-cock" announces a startled grouse. The bubbling jubilant cry of the golden plover—inseparable, somehow, from a raw wind and snow water—comes to him off the uplands. Often he happens on the body of a sheep, partly eaten, jammed in a rock crevice beside an eddy. And sometimes, in topping a rise, he may surprise a stag, standing a few yards off at a burn entrance, sombre-eyed, his rank red winter coat etched harshly against the snow.

Always, in highland or lowland, there is that fascinating and more immediate attraction, the salmon. Here is a study which will never be exhausted, and in which the behaviour of individuals confounds continually any attempt at logic. The fisherman will meet the salmon as others have met it: the salmon that takes the bait, and the salmon that runs away from it as though it had horns and hooves; the salmon that moves sulkily away at the sight of a line or a fisherman, and yet takes readily after a tree has crashed into the river close by or chips from a near-by rock blast have torn

4

the pool like a burst of shrapnel; the hooked salmon that sulks at the bottom, and the hooked salmon that hurls itself about like a mad thing, even throwing itself into a bush or against a cliff.

The fisherman may never catch a forty-pounder. He may, on the other hand, if he fishes the Tweed or the Aaro, beat the British and Norwegian records of 69¾ lb. and 69½ lb., which were made respectively in those two rivers. He may fish for a fortnight and never catch a fish; or he may take, as Mr Naylor did on the Grimersta in 1888, fifty-four salmon in a single day— though the likelihood of a record bag is less than that of a record fish.

Wherever and however long a man fishes for salmon, he will find much to learn and much to contradict. For many things he will find a reason. For many he will think he has found a reason, until the salmon, pre-occupied and indifferent, gives him to start his cycles of thought all over again. However much he learns, there will still be times when he finds the salmon be-having in ways for which there is no accounting, ways not explained in any book, the reason for which not even the salmon knows, but only that Force which drives it ever upwards to those clear springs where it received and must pass on the vehicle of life.

CHAPTER II

THE SALMON FISHERMAN'S DEAD RECKONING

> There's mony a water, great or sma',
>   Gaes singing in his siller tune,
> Through glen and heugh, and hope and shaw,
>   Beneath the sunlicht or the moon.
>   ANDREW LANG, *Ballade of the Tweed*

His first sight of a pool in a great Highland salmon
river is a thing that a keen fisherman will remember
all his days. There is a grandeur about a big salmon
pool that is unsurpassed by any other sight on earth.
The white surges at the head, so far off that their shout-
ing comes to his ears simply as a dull drift of sound,
the immense black dub, fifty, sixty, perhaps a hundred,
yards across, creaming and eddying till its current
passes into the boulder-studded tail and, far below,
gathers speed again for the next plunge—there is so
much water and it moves so majestically that to come
and dangle a line in it seems an impertinence.

If the intending salmon fisherman has previously
caught only trout, his admiration will probably soon
change to a feeling akin to despair. Where, in all that
magnificence, are the salmon? How are they to be
caught? The bank of rounded pebbles, dazzling white,
on which the fisherman stands, slopes into amber
water, and vanishes, not ten yards out, into depths at
which he can only guess. A trout hangs in the sunlit
"broo", just opposite, rising busily to a hatch of duns.
There is a simple problem! A rod and a floating fly,

6

and the fisherman need not bother about temperature, time of year, or anything, in fact, except placing the fly a little above the trout's nose. That is all he has to do, and the chances are that the trout is his.

But he is salmon fishing. Far out above the surface of the pool—so far that the splash it makes is not discernible—a salmon, flashing silver, appears and disappears, coming God knows whence and going God knows whither. Why did it jump like that? Was it after food, like the homely trout? And where is it now, in all that mass of water? What is the fisherman, standing so small on the great bank of shingle, going to do to catch it? His eyes tell him only that it has come and gone again, inscrutable as the smiling surface of the pool, wherein afterwards, as in the air that the eagle passed through, "no sign where she went is to be found".

Because the evidence of his eyes, however long he might stand looking at the river, would tell the salmon fisherman practically nothing about how to catch salmon, the first thing he must do is to use the accumulated experience of others to work out, as a seaman does, a sort of dead reckoning.

The first part of this calculation is done before going to the river. In leasing a river it should be done even before the lease is signed. It consists in finding out *when the salmon are likely to be there*! One must never lose sight of the fact that salmon are migratory fish. They come and they go, and there are many times when excellent stretches of most salmon rivers *contain no salmon at all*. The first and most important things to discover, therefore, are whether the river is "early" or "late", how far the particular beat aimed at is from the sea, and whether there is anything to induce the salmon to stop in it, or whether they are in the habit of running straight through.

7

"Early", in this connection, is an approximate term, and is applied to a river in which the main run of fish occurs, say, before the end of February; while the "late" river may be said to be one in which the main run takes place during March or April. But it is well, before embarking on a lease, to make quite sure when the runs of the previous year or two occurred.

Generally speaking, the spring is the best time to catch salmon in the British Isles. In many rivers there is a second run in the autumn,—generally at some time during the months of September and October—but this is a much smaller affair than the spring run. In Canadian rivers the big run is rather later, May and June being the best months, and Norwegian rivers are later still, melting snow and ice retarding the best fish until about July.

In most rivers the run is a definite affair lasting only a couple of weeks—although salmon continue to come in in small numbers all through the summer—and rain generally advances it, while drought delays it. So that the weather in these early months has also to be taken into account in estimating the stock of salmon.

A beat near the sea will hold salmon earlier in the year than a beat far up the river. But a beat near the sea is not always an advantage, because the salmon sometimes run too quickly through it—as they do, for instance, in the lower reaches of the Aberdeenshire Dee. If a prospective beat is near the sea, one should find out if there is anything in it to hold the salmon up. A beat with plenty of cover in it in the shape of rocks and well-defined pools, and a weir or a difficult fall at its upper end is far more likely to be a good proposition than one through which the salmon can run easily, with no inducement to rest on the way.

These four considerations, then, the time of year,

8

the amount of rain, the general physical appearance of the beat, and its distance from the sea, enable the fisherman to gain a shrewd idea whether there are any salmon in his beat or not. Of course, in many places, the pools are of such a kind that most of the salmon in them can be seen, and on most rivers information about the size of the previous week's bags on adjoining beats will indicate the state of affairs in that to which the fisherman intends to go. In either of those cases, of course, this preliminary part of his dead reckoning is made very much easier.

Assuming that the beat contains salmon, the other matters to decide are whereabouts in each pool they are likely to be, what method is most likely to catch them, and at what time of day and state of weather they are most likely to be caught.

In working out whereabouts in a pool a salmon is likely to be, the first thing to remember is that the chief business of the salmon in fresh water is not to feed, but to breed. Its main preoccupation is to get upstream to the spawning grounds as fast as possible. Practically all its feeding, once it has reached the smolt stage, is done in the sea. In the river it is, first and foremost, a traveller. It stops on the way only because it is tired, or because it is held up by some obstacle, such as a weir or a fall, which is either too high or has too little water coming over it to allow it to pass. A salmon's place in the pool, therefore, will be in water which is quiet enough to allow it to lie comfortably and which, at the same time, is deep enough to give it cover. Four feet is about the minimum depth in which a salmon seems to feel happy, and as at this and greater depths the slackest water is that nearest the bottom, that is where the salmon will be.

It is clear, then, that the mid-water stations, whence

9

a dart can be made at a morsel of food sweeping past in the current, the eddies, in which the jetsam of the stream is dumped, and the shady hovers beneath the trees or the bank, from which flies and grubs drop periodically, are of no interest at all to the salmon. The trout fisherman, now in pursuit of bigger game, must learn to look at the pool from an entirely new standpoint. He must see in the surface of the pool not those variations which indicate a station where a fish can feed, but those which indicate an "ease", where it can lie.

The latter task is much the harder of the two. In fact it is often impossible to deduce, from the appearance of the surface currents, the features at the bottom which are likely to appeal to a salmon. It is here that local knowledge is of such immense help. *A salmon fisherman should always rely upon people who know the river, in preference to his own judgment, to tell him where salmon lie.* To illustrate both the soundness of the former and the uncertainty of the latter I cannot do better than quote an experience recounted by Percy Nobbs in the delightful book which he calls *Salmon Tactics*: "Well above the head of the Medway there is a featureless widening of the river. I was about to pass down one windy day, when my boatman said, 'You'll get a fish here if anywhere'. I said 'Where?' incredulously. Jim then pointed to a bush on the other side, and told me to get out a long line, which I did. 'Some more', he demanded, and again 'Some more'. Then 'Three feet more . . . and strike!' And there I was, into a fine fish. There happened to be a sunken sharp-edged ledge and that ledge had a nick in it and that nick made a salmon 'lie'; and the ledge being razor-backed, made no sign on the surface as a flat or round-backed ledge or rock would do."

Often a "taking place" in an apparently featureless

pool is explained by there being a patch of flat rock in the bottom at that point, on which the salmon like to lie, resting on their pectoral fins.

Where local knowledge is available, always rely on it. Where it is not, one has to try and deduce the configuration of the bottom from the appearance of the surface.

No two salmon pools are the same. The anatomy of a pool will depend on the rate of fall of the river at that particular point and on the nature of its bed. Where a river falls slowly, whether it be through high peat flats or flowering lowland meads, the pools are apt to be dull, canal-like affairs, generally deep, with a small, gentle run at the head, and a long featureless stretch of almost still water. It might be imagined, from what has been said above, that this quiet water would be ideal. But it does not follow. Salmon are apt to run through such a place, unless it lies immediately above a length of steep, difficult water. One has to keep constantly in mind that the one idea of a salmon in fresh water is to push on upstream to the spawning grounds as fast as possible, and that it stops only to rest and recruit its energies for the next stage of its journey. Flat, dead water is rarely much good to the fisherman, and if it does happen to contain salmon the still surface gives no indication where they will lie.

The most usual type of salmon pool is one where the river is falling faster. It enters the throat in a strong surging rush, spreads and steadies into a heavy central portion, often called the "dub", from which it passes into the "tail" which is the slowest part of the pool, and then gathers speed once more in a smooth "glide" preparatory to entering the throat of the next pool.

If such a pool has plenty of eases in it, such as deepish quiet water on the edge of the rush and boulders in the dub and tail, salmon will probably stop there. The essentials are that the salmon should, on entering the pool, feel the heavy water, and then at once be able to find convenient shelter, where they can rest before tackling it.

The surges in the throat of a pool are worth fishing only in drought conditions, when the fish come up and hang there in order to get oxygen. But sometimes the head of the pool consists of two or three more or less separate streams. A shingle bank or an outcrop of rock divides the inflow, making a strong central rush and one or more gentler, smaller rushes, which one may call "stickles". If these are of a fair depth themselves or fall into deep pots or rock faults, they will often hold salmon, especially in the summer months. But as a general rule the eases lower down the pool are the places to look for.

The dub, to the fisherman without local knowledge, is usually an enigma. The water is too deep and too swirly to indicate at the surface the presence of sub-merged rocks, behind which the salmon might be lying. One just has to fish the whole of it, paying particular attention to anything that looks like a rock "boil" and to the water behind points of rock which jut out from the bank.

The tail of the pool is generally shallower than the dub, and submerged rocks can be spotted by the boils and riffles they make in the more evenly-flowing surface. A rock is well upstream of the boil which it makes, not immediately underneath it. The distance of the rock upstream of its boil is approximately three times the depth of water over the top of the rock. If the depth over the top of the rock is four feet, the rock will be four yards upstream of the boil. A bait or a fly, cast into the boil, would, therefore, go nowhere near the salmon. It is, of course, impossible to make an accurate estimate of the depth of water over a rock, but where the rock is obviously well below the surface, as where there is simply a boil without any appreciable hump in the water, the fly or bait should be made to land well above the boil.

The "glide", where the water from the tail of the pool begins to gather speed for its plunge into the next rush, often provides the best lie in the pool. If there

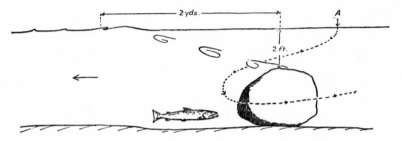

A diagram to show the deductions from a rock boil. If the depth of water over the top of the rock is estimated at 2 feet, then the rock will be about 2 yards upstream of the boil and the fish will be lying probably within a yard of the rock. The fly or bait should be made to alight at A, so that it will have had time to sink by the time it enters the eddy behind the rock.

are any rocks in it, these will be the first the salmon come to after surmounting the rapids below, and if it is of a fair depth, with an uneven bottom, eases form in it without the agency of rocks. The water seems to trip on the bottom and make small patches of stillness well below the surface. I remember watching a salmon in the Irfon above Llangamarch lying motionless on its fins at the bottom of a smooth tearing rush between one pool and the next. The water at the surface was moving at seven or eight knots, while at the bottom, in the particular spot where the salmon lay, it must have been practically still. There is seldom any indication on the surface of a glide to show this reverse current. One can only say that if the glide is obviously deep, it is worth fishing, even though it apparently contains no rocks or ease of any kind.

Difference in the height of water will, of course, alter the position of the lies, but the same rules for finding them hold good. During a flood, the increased volume of water will obliterate some eases, while others are formed nearer the bank or farther down the tail of the pool, in places that were formerly too shallow or too still. But a big flood as a rule is not a time to fish, because the salmon are running. The increased volume of water gives them a chance to surmount obstacles, which in a normal height would be impassable, owing to the water coming over being too shallow or too full of air bubbles to give the fish the purchase that they need. When salmon are running they are not inclined to take a bait.

The other main factor that determines the position of salmon in a pool is the oxygen content of the water. This depends on the temperature, which in turn corresponds roughly to the time of year. When the water is very cold, as in early spring, the salmon will be in the deeper, quieter places, moving up into the streams only when a spell of fine weather raises the temperature of the river. In drought conditions salmon will lie in the very throats of the pools, wherever they can find some ease beneath the rush. But, in whatever part of the pool they may be, they prefer to lie on the bottom rather than hang in mid-water.

Having arrived at an approximate idea whereabouts in the pool the salmon are likely to be, the next thing to consider is what bait to offer them. And that brings us at once to the vexed question: Do salmon feed while they are in the river?

I may as well say at once that I think the *minutiae* of this question are of far more importance to the scientist than they are to the fisherman. It is common knowledge that a salmon will at times take a bunch of worms or a prawn, and that food has occasionally, if very rarely, been found in the stomachs of salmon which had been a long time in a river. At the same time the experience of every salmon fisherman has soon led him to suspect that the satisfaction of hunger forms such a very small part of a salmon's preoccupation while it is in the river that it cannot be relied on, as he relies on this motive in a trout, to determine what bait he should use.

A salmon loses weight in the river, using the fat which it has accumulated in the sea to form its eggs or milt, as the case may be, and also to give it energy to travel up to the spawning grounds. Certainly it does not rely on the food it can find in the river to keep itself alive. If it did, it would be found in mid-water and in the feeding stations where the trout are, rising steadily on a warm evening to the hatches of fly, or be seen chasing trout, after the manner of a pike; instead of which it spends most of its time, when not actually travelling, in resting quietly on the bottom. The frequent leaps in which the salmon indulges may be attempts to free itself of, say, lice or other parasites; but they certainly cannot be interpreted as serious efforts to take surface flies. Once in a blue moon a salmon will rise steadily and quietly at a hatch of fly, but the point is, if it relied on fresh-water food it would do this *as often as the trout.* The fact that a salmon's stomach is generally found to be empty—so often adduced as evidence that it does not feed in fresh water—can be explained by the rapidity of its digestion and its habit of disgorging the contents of its stomach as soon as it is hooked. But

15

direct evidence of its behaviour in the river, so far as that has been observed, and the circumstance that it loses its feeding teeth shortly before it arrives there both point to the probability that a salmon feeds only on very rare occasions while it is in the river, and then only in a capricious and uncertain manner.

The object, therefore, must be to stir the salmon out of its apathy, preoccupation, depression, or whatever is the state of mind which prevents it from hunting for food while it is in the river. This may either be done by offering it something specially tempting in the way of a *bonne bouche*, such as a fly fished with a slack line, a prawn, or a worm, for there is still that odd chance of its taking a natural bait (though what it imagines a drifting salmon fly to be passes comprehension); or it may be done by offering it something calculated to arouse feelings akin to curiosity, hunting instinct, or annoyance, such as a rapidly moving fly or a spinning bait.

The choice of the kind of bait (and by "bait" I include "fly") will depend to some extent on the height of the water, but chiefly on one's own personal preference. Fly fishing is generally considered the pleasantest way of taking salmon, with spinning, which was formerly rather despised, now a close second. Since the advent of the greased line and the thread line, fly fishing and spinning are practically interchangeable, and are of equal use at almost any time of year and state of water, except a thick flood. Because they are both considered pleasanter ways of fishing than either prawning or worming, they are more often employed. But if two fishermen were allotted beats of equal value, and one fished throughout the season with only fly and spinning baits, the other only with prawn and worm, the latter would probably end up with as many fish as the former. The worm is especially useful in very thick water, as the salmon can find it by smell when it or any other bait is invisible. The prawn is more generally useful in low water.

Such preference as the salmon have—and it is often very marked—is, as far as we know at present, a matter of pure caprice. Probably it arises out of some particular condition or set of conditions external to the salmon itself, because the fish throughout a whole beat so often display exactly the same preference or aversion simultaneously. One day they will all be mad for prawn; another day a prawn will actually terrify them. One day they will come well to both fly and spinner; another day, under apparently exactly the same conditions, they will not look at either.

Sometimes the terms of the licence or lease restrict the fisherman to some particular kind of bait—generally the fly—either throughout the season or for some part of it. The idea behind this is that the other ways of fishing bore or scare salmon to a greater extent than fly fishing and would spoil the water for the next fisherman. But it has nothing whatever to do with their efficiency. When no such restriction is in force, the only things to bear in mind, when deciding what kind of bait to use, are that a spinning bait is more likely to succeed after a fly than a fly is after a spinner, that a spinning bait can be cast farther than a fly and made to sink deeper, so that it can fish water which a fly could not, that a worm is useful in very thick water, and that a prawn should only be used as a last resort, as it is apt to scare salmon out of a pool altogether. Apart from these considerations, the fisherman need not be afraid that he is losing anything by using the method that he happens to enjoy best.

The size of bait is quite another matter. It is vastly

17

important. Temperature affects it, as also do the height of water, the depth of water in any particular pool, and the light, not only of the sky, but that reflected in the pool itself. Cold water demands a big bait, because in cold water salmon are less lively than they are in warm, and so a bigger bait is needed to stir them out of their lethargy. In water which is thick or deep a big bait is more visible than a small one; and this same consideration recommends a big bait on a day which is dull or in a pool which has a dark floor or is heavily shaded by rocks or trees. Conversely, water which is warm, clear, or shallow, a day that is sunny, or a pool that is open and bright, demands a small bait.

Temperature will also decide whether a bait should be fished at the bottom or at the surface. If the air is colder than the water, a fish will not come up and the bait must be fished right down on the stones. If the air is warmer than the water, the fish will come up to a fly fished at or just under the surface. In the latter conditions a spinning bait would no doubt be taken at the surface as well as a fly, but it is seldom used because a fly is lighter and so more easily kept from sinking. Wooden plug baits or "wigglers", which float, and do not spin, but wobble, when drawn through the water, can be worked like a surface fly, and would, I imagine, be equally attractive, whenever the temperature of the air exceeded that of the water.

The position of the sun, quite apart from its intensity, is another matter which has to be taken into account, especially in deciding what water to fish and where to cast from. For two reasons the sun shining up the path of the bait is better for fishing than the sun shining down it. The fish lie with their heads pointing upstream, and the bait comes down or down and across. Light behind them illumines the bait, which is being

18

floated in front of them. A light in front of them makes nothing but a silhouette of the bait and at the same

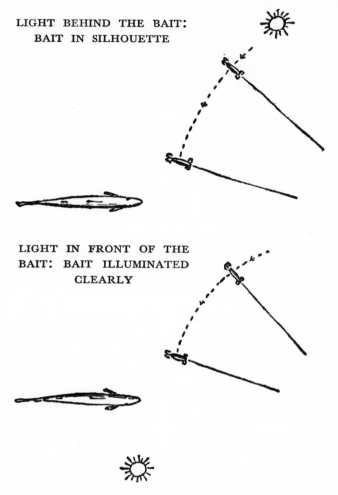

LIGHT BEHIND THE BAIT:
BAIT IN SILHOUETTE

LIGHT IN FRONT OF THE
BAIT: BAIT ILLUMINATED
CLEARLY

time dazzles the fish. For these reasons, a low evening sun shining directly down the path of the bait generally makes fishing hopeless. For the same reasons it is best to cast from the bank from which the sun is shining; the path of the bait is across and down from the far bank to one's own, and light from behind one shines across this path, whereas light from the other bank would shine down it. I am sure that the success which so often results from changing the angle of cast is due to the better illumination of the bait when worked from the new angle.

Fog, *per se*, has far less effect on salmon fishing than it has on trout fishing. The reduced light may mean a bigger bait, but it is the temperature that matters. Fog is only the *result* of a change of temperature, not the cause of it. The mist, that so often forms after a hot day late in the year, results from rapid cooling of the air. The fish may not come up any longer after it appears, but the reason lies not in the visible presence of the mist, but in the fact that the air has become cooler than the water. The same applies to the lengthier mani-festations—Scotch mist, "haar", etc. In every case, the comparison between the temperatures of air and water is what matters.

While the best time of year for salmon fishing is un-doubtedly the spring, when the salmon have been only a day or two in the river and seem still to retain the feeding habit, the best time of day will depend on the time of year. Up to the end of March when the days are still short, the middle of the day, between 11 A.M. and 3 P.M., is the best time. Light and warmth in the midst of dark and cold wake salmon up, as they do everything else. Later on, the hot weather causes a slack period between about 1 P.M. and 4 P.M. The best times are then between 11 A.M. and 1 P.M. and between 4 P.M. and sunset. In the long July days when the river is often very low and clear there is often a good patch early in the morning between say 6 A.M. and 8 A.M., especially just as the sun begins really to warm up the air.

In approaching the pool, should one take any trouble to keep out of sight, as one does when trout fishing? Can such an indifferent-seeming beast as a salmon be disturbed by the approach of a kind of being whom it has probably never seen and so certainly does not connect with danger? I think the answer to both these questions is: Yes. A salmon may not actually be *frightened* by such portents as a fisherman's legs and wading staff, or a flash from a piece of thick gut near the attractive bait, but it can be distracted or disturbed by these things. Generally the din of the river and the turmoil of the water will provide cover for the fisherman himself, but salmon have marvellous sight, and it pays to fish fine, and to move as carefully as possible in quiet places.

One more consideration completes the fisherman's dead reckoning. How many separate outfits should be taken down to the river? Should one take as little as possible or as much as one can carry? To that I say, take as many different outfits as your own patience or that of your gillie will stand. It is impossible to tell beforehand exactly what one may need or to pin one's faith to any single outfit. Changes of light, of temperature, of height of water, and often of sheer difficulty of ground may necessitate complete change of method. It may seem a good fly day, yet the fish may refuse a fly. A pool that cannot be fished with a fly, because it is too wide or the water is too deep and strong for the fly to be sunk to the bottom, may be ideal for spinning. The very change in the size of fly between throat and dub, or dub and tail, may mean a change of rod and line.

A trout fisherman cannot indulge on the same day in

21

fishing with more than one outfit, except where he is fishing from a boat, for he has farther to go, and seldom takes an attendant. But salmon fishing is a more stationary business. It may take a couple of hours to fish even a single pool, and if the spare gear is left on the bank or in the hut it may be reached in a very few minutes. So that to take several outfits to the river and make full use of them, even if one is alone, is not so impossible as might appear. And a change in good time may mean the fish of one's dreams. Spare gear is always a nuisance, but salmon fishing is too expensive a ship to be spoiled for a ha'porth of tar.

River Dee,
at Cairnton.

The Nyth,
River Wye.

River Tummel,
above Logierait.

"BETWEEN LOWLAND AND HIGHLAND"

Three pleasant stretches with a gentle fall and well-defined pools. The lower one is broad enough to make a boat an advantage.

A POOL ON THE TUMMEL BELOW GUAY, IN LOW WATER AND SPATE

This is a typical case of a pool which is fairly well defined, yet which has little
to indicate the lies of the fish. With the water at the height shown in the upper
photograph the whole run is fishable, from the upper end of the whaleback down
to the water in the foreground, the salmon lying mostly towards the near bank.

The lower photograph shows the water too high to make fishing possible in this
part of the pool.

CHAPTER III

FIXED ASSETS

The twelfth and last of all is Memory,
Remembering well before he setteth out,
Each needful thing that he must occupy;
And not to stand of any want in doubt.
Or leave something behind forgetfully:
When he hath walked the fields and brooks about,
  It were a grief back to return again,
  For things forgot that should his sport maintain.
          JOHN DENNYS, *The Secrets of Angling*

THERE are certain things that the salmon fisherman must possess, quite apart from the special gear that any particular method demands. Many of them are small things, but without any one of them the day's fishing may be, if not ruined, at any rate made less pleasant.

Let us talk first about waders, as they are much the most important part of the salmon fisherman's permanent gear. Leg waders are not much use to the fisherman who wants to catch salmon. They are all very well for the trout fisherman, who rarely has to go into more than a foot or two of water; but in salmon fishing the casts are much longer, and in order to cover the water it is often important to go in as deep as you can. To be able to stand in 3 feet 6 inches of water may often mean reaching fish which would have been out of range if your limit had only been 2 feet. Buy trouser waders, therefore, and let them come right up to the armpits.

The fit of waders is vitally important. You will be

23

spending the whole day in them, and in addition to the underwater hazards there will be fences to get over and possibly cliffs and banks to climb, and your frame of mind, if your waders fit properly, will be better suited to these manœuvres than it will if there is a wrinkle under the sole of your foot or a splitting noise in the region of your braces every time you bend your knee.

The feet of waders should fit just comfortably over a pair of thick stockings. If any latitude is allowed it should be over the instep, to simplify putting on and taking off. Unless your gillie has served in a cavalry regiment, or been valet to a M.F.H., he will probably object to co-operating in the only possible method of removing tight waders. Do not have them free enough, though, to run any risk of forming a wrinkle. Wrinkles, besides being uncomfortable, cause chafe and let the water through in a very short time. The fit above the knee, on the other hand, can be much slacker, with the crutch cut high so that you can get over stiles in comfort. The top should be cut like the mouth of a sack, slack enough to give ample room for an elbow when you want to get something out of a trouser pocket. The whole garment should be supported by broad web straps crossed in front as well as behind, as this arrangement contributes greatly towards making the pockets accessible.

Brogues are as important as waders. I have never found anything to beat canvas and leather as materials for brogues. The leather provides a stiff protection for the foot and the canvas strips in the upper make it flexible. Protection for the feet is essential, where you are knocking about amongst boulders and jags of rock that you cannot even see. Rubber does not give this. Not being stiff, pressure goes straight through it.

Rubber shoes, to be thick enough to give proper protection, would have to be made a good deal heavier than leather, so the advantage of lightness which is often claimed for them is ruled out. Boots, too, are better than shoes, as they support the ankles—an important point when you cannot see where you are treading.

Don't be afraid of getting good heavy brogues. Weight is not nearly such an important consideration to the salmon fisherman as it is to the trout fisherman. The latter may have to walk ten or fifteen miles in a day, while the former seldom moves more than two, and stands much more of his time in the water, where weight does not matter. Protection is the most important thing to consider in choosing brogues. The fit should be a comfortable fit over (1) a pair of thick stockings, (2) waders, and (3) a pair of very thick wading socks. See, particularly, that there is plenty of room in the toes. The best brogues I ever owned were bought in the Black Forest one summer when I was after trout. They were made by a Zurich firm and had bulbous toes of stiff leather like a Rugger boot. And they were prodigiously comfortable.

I think that a leather sole well filled with big soft hob-nails is probably the safest for all-round work. The nails wear down quickly and want renewing. Soak the sole before driving in fresh ones, so as not to start the others out of the leather. In old days on the Dart I used to use a compressed felt sole. The Double Dart is a fearsome place to fish, and that was the only stuff I could find that would grip on smooth, slippery rock. In fact it grips splendidly on everything except wet grass, and has the further advantage of not making a noise ; but it is expensive and wears, of course, very much more quickly than a hob-nailed sole.

25

Do not on any account buy brogues fitted with hooks for the laces, as the lace of one brogue may catch on one of the hooks of the other whilst you are wading and lock your feet together—bad enough at any time, but in strong or deep water a really dreadful predicament. This danger is pretty generally realised now, and most manufacturers fit their brogues with eyelet-holes.

With the waders described above, the only further waterproofing one needs is a very short macintosh jacket and a gabardine deerstalker or a sou'wester; but if you have a sou'wester, let it be black, not yellow.

Some sort of staff for wading is often a very present help in time of trouble. If you use it as a gaff handle as well you save carrying a gaff about separately, and get the additional advantage of having a really long handle. Whole cane is enormously strong, but it is hollow and eventually rots inside and may one day let you down. A stout piece of hazel or ash about 5 feet long, like a Boy Scout's stave is as good as anything. It should be well varnished and fitted at the butt end with a rubber ferrule—not a metal spike, as this makes an appalling noise (much greater, for some reason, than one's hob-nailed brogues) on the stones under water. It should be fixed securely with a rivet. I find that a rubber rod-button, screwed into a socket and then secured with a rivet, makes a splendid end fitting for a wading staff.

The gaff or tailer should be *lashed* to the upper end— not screwed in, as the screw is apt to loosen on gaffing a fish and create confusion. The lashing can be made with a leather bootlace or a piece of waxed twine, and a good finish for it is shown in the diagram. The hook of the gaff itself should consist of a plain round bend, *not* a sort of shepherd's crook, and should be not less than $3\frac{1}{2}$ inches in the gape. The point should be straight, parallel to the shank, and literally as sharp as a needle.

It should be protected by a cork or a piece of wood, bound with sticky tape to stop it splitting and attached to the shaft by a short length of twine. It may seem a refinement of caution to suggest painting the gaff a dark green, but I have seen fish sheer away from a bright gaff and I think they did so because it *was* bright.

It is impossible to sling a long-handled gaff in any of the ways that a telescopic gaff can be slung, but

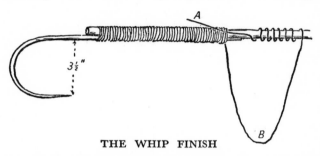

THE WHIP FINISH

As the left-hand part of the loop B is wound tightly over the end A to finish the binding, the right-hand part unwinds itself from the staff. When all these loose turns are gone, the end A is pulled tight and snipped off.

it is a nuisance without an attachment of some sort which will leave your hands free. A simple and useful sling can be made out of a small curtain ring—small enough not to slip over the button at the end of the staff—and a thin leather strap or a piece of blind-cord. Both ends of the strap are attached to the ring so that it forms a loop rather more than a yard long, and the ring is passed on to the shaft by way of the hook and the loop slipped over your shoulder. Whatever you want to do with the gaff, the loop and the ring need never be taken off. In wading, the loop is long enough to give free play to the staff, and, in gaffing, it is long enough, when the ring is slipped down to the button, to allow the gaff to be extended to the full reach of your arm. While standing in the water and casting, the ring is slipped down to the button and the gaff allowed to float and trail in the water. For roughly slinging the gaff when standing in shallow water or on dry land, one can lash the two parts of

GAFF AND SLING

the loop together about half-way up the loop, and lash a clip rather more than half-way up the gaff. The gaff can then be hooked on to the rear upper part of the loop, and hangs more or less vertically behind the left shoulder.

If you must use a telescopic gaff, see that the hook has a gape of proper size and is sharp. Pocket gaffs made out of cod-hooks I never could see the use of.

28

One can only gaff a fish with them in the worst possible place, the jaw, which leaves its whole body free to thrash about; and to do even that one has to bring the fish to within about 9 inches of one's hand—in many places a physical impossibility.

A tailer usually takes the form of a running noose, the standing part of which is composed of some springy substance like whalebone and is made fast to a wooden handle. The loop is passed over the tail of the fish and given a sharp jerk, when the traveller slips down the whalebone and the noose springs tight. A tailer is perhaps even more useful than a gaff, as a gaff is forbidden on many rivers in the spring when the kelts are coming down, and a tailer, besides being then the only thing to use as a substitute, is at all times an efficient weapon and has the advantage of giving kelts the benefit of the doubt.

In whatever way one may be fishing a cast case is always necessary. One is practically always needing gut, and even if, when spinning, one sticks grimly to wire, there are some important little matters quite apart from gut which must stow in the cast case and which I shall now describe.

Number One is a stick of carborundum for keeping hook points sharp. Only the tiniest piece is needed, and it should be of medium gauge and shaped either flat, or round like a pencil, so as to stick into a leather loop in the flap of the cast case. Number Two is a pair of scissors, sharp, with fine points; and Numbers Three, Four, and Five, for emergency rod repairs, are respectively, a piece of sticky tape, packed flat, a piece of waxed twine, and some slivers of wood or watch-spring.

These things take up very little room in the cast case, the pattern of which does not greatly matter. My own

4

is a rather large old pigskin notecase, with two pockets, on one of which I have sewn a strip of pigskin to take the scissors and the carborundum.

A knife is a thing that one will always need sooner or later. It must have at any rate one strong sharp blade. As to additional fittings, a stiletto is occasionally useful, and also a hook scale engraved on the frame. A corkscrew in the knife is *very* useful. I do not like a knife equipped with a pair of scissors—it is a niggling little fitting with a spring in it, and it always seems to go rusty. I can remember to oil reels and even hooks and swivels, but the knife somehow seems too common-place to deserve such attention—with the result that the scissors rust and seize up.

A piece of blind-cord and a few wire paper-clips are invaluable for improvising fish carriers and tackle releasers. I shall describe these devices later on.

A priest is a handier thing than one might imagine. I used not to carry one, until I realised what an awkward business it is trying to kill a salmon with a stone or a gaff handle. One should try to make as neat a job as possible of putting a fish out of its discomfort and fright—I will not say pain, for I do not believe a salmon feels pain as we understand it. There are many excellent little priests on the market. The smallest size that will do the work weighs about 9 ounces and should be short enough to slip easily into a coat pocket.

Our ancestors would have smiled at the idea of taking out a thermometer for comparing the temperatures of water and air, but the importance of these factors in determining whether a fly should be fished at the surface or at the bottom cannot be overestimated. A thermometer is the only certain means of discovering them, and a salmon fisherman should never go out without one. It is a tiny thing, about the size of a

Above: A CLEAN SALMON AND A PROPER GAFF

Below: ALMOST A KELT: AN AUTUMN COCK FISH
JUST BEFORE SPAWNING

A SQUARE CAST ON THE WARREN

Fishing the head of the Church Pool on the Warren, near Hay, Hereford. The fly is being thrown across the fast water into the ease on the far side of the run. This picture also shows how a long gaff should be slung.

fountain pen, housed in a metal shield and fitted with a clip so that it can be hooked into an inside pocket.

A rough leather glove is useful in spring for un-hooking kelts, which have teeth like needles. In tailing by hand, too, it gives one a surer grip of the fish.

If one takes one's fishing at all seriously, a pencil and some sort of note-book or card come in handy for noting down details of fish caught. The most important things to note—much more important than the size of the fish or the pattern of the fly—are the date, the time of day, the light, the height and temperature of the water, the *size* of the fly or bait, and the place in the pool where the fish took hold. It is a finicking business, I know, to write all these solemnly down, when the salmon are in the humour and your time is short, but by doing so you remind yourself of the influences which really control fishing and soon form a habit of taking them automatically into account.

Flask, tobacco, and matches—in a waterproof case—completes the list of fixed assets that should be taken into the water.

The total weight of these things, not including waders and gaff, need not exceed $2\frac{3}{4}$ lb. (including an allow-ance of 22 oz. for the flask and its contents), and they will stow easily into two coat pockets.

A bag is unnecessary, except for holding spare tackle, minnows, etc., when it should be left on the bank. Nor do you need a spring balance. It is a heavy thing and can be left at home. The salmon will not have shrunk by the time you get back. Mr Arthur Hutton has shown that the loss of weight in a salmon within twelve hours of being caught is negligible. Immediate curi-osity, however, can be satisfied by nothing more com-plicated than a tape measure. Measure the maximum girth of the salmon and its length from the nose to the fork of the tail. Then

$$\frac{\text{Girth squared (in inches)} \times \text{length (in inches)}}{800} = \text{weight of the fish in lb.}$$

This is a most accurate formula, better than any scale depending on length alone, as by including the girth measurement it makes allowance for the condition of the fish.

Anti-fly dope and clothing in Iceland, Finland, and Canada, and sometimes in Norway and Scotland, is a question on the solution of which one's very sanity may depend. I do not believe there is any dope made that will keep flies away when they are really out for blood, though some of the many modern proprietary repellents are better than the old sweet-smelling remedies like oil of lavender or oil of white birch, which the hosts of the enemy seemed positively to enjoy. A pipe is useless; the ranker the tobacco, the better they like it.

If flies look like being at all bad, it is best to make sure of one's comfort at once by covering up as much of one's hands and head as possible. Mr Percy Nobbs, in his delightful book *Salmon Tactics*, describes a way of doing this which is at once so simple and excellent that it saddens me to think of the agony I might have been saved, on more than one occasion, had I had the sense to think of it myself. "The wrists", he says, "are best protected by old shirt-sleeves with the cuffs cut off, and elastic at both ends. The lower elastic should just fit the hand above the fingers, and a hole behind the elastic must be provided for the thumb. The upper band is best placed above the elbow. Out of the back of an old shirt one can make a light 'Balaclava helmet' with a deep skirt to go inside the collar of the shirt one wears, and a small face-hole from the eyebrows to the

32

middle of the chin. Thus equipped one need only dope the fingers and the cheek-bones."

While we are on this subject of permanent fixtures, it may be worth mentioning those that are left at home. For storing fishing gear one needs various boxes, cabinets, or what you will, but rods, if left set up, should be stowed on shelves, *not* on pegs. A hook-gut-and-line scale is useful, especially if you are given to making up your own casts. You can then be really sure of the sizes and strengths you want to use.

An oil-can full of some thin oil such as 3-in-1, for reels, swivels, hooks, and wire, should be purchased and kept in a safe, of which only yourself has the key. Competition for the single oil can that belongs either to you or to your wife's sewing machine is the beginning of the end.

A line drier puts beyond the pale of possibility such awful moments as when a terrier leaps into the chair in which you have laid the coils of your wet line. A line drier *should not wobble.* It is more excellent still if the frame travels from side to side on a threaded spindle as the line is being wound on to it, so that the line is spaced evenly on the bars.

A rod-box of five-eighths oak, measuring inside 5 feet 6 inches by 3 inches by 4 inches, fitted with sunk brass corners from an old gun-case and heavy sunk brass hinges, and capable of holding five rods and a wading staff, can be made by yourself or the local carpenter for half of what you would pay a tackle-maker for a deal-and-iron one. A tubular fabric case is lighter and saves air freight; but, sooner or later, even in these days, a fishing journey may mean rail and ship, without the option of a car. It is then that the heart of oak will keep your own heart out of your mouth when you see your possessions, in the bottom of the luggage net, being dropped on to a stone quay beneath a ton and a half of sharp-edged trunks.

CHAPTER IV

THE DELICATE ART OF WADING

Keep your head and feet dry, for from the offence of them
springeth Agues, and worse informities.
GERVASE MARKHAM, *Country Contentments*

WADING is the beginning and the end of salmon fishing.
Nine times out of ten a fisherman wades before he
makes the first cast of his life for a salmon, and after the
fly has come home for the last time there is nothing
left for him but to wade ashore again—unless indeed he
has the fortune, as Lord Trevethin did, who was the
most gallant, and perhaps the finest, salmon fisherman
in Europe, to make his end at a ripe old age in the
waters which he has come to love as his own fireside.

Wading is a delicate and a dangerous art, and the
first essential to its successful practice is comfort. Never
wade without waders. That game simply is not worth
the candle. It may seem pleasant on a long hot
summer's day to stand in cold water, but after a very
short time it is neither comfortable nor safe. Do not be
deluded into thinking that it does not matter how wet
or cold you get so long as you have a hot bath and
change immediately on reaching home. That applies
only when shooting or hunting or doing something
which keeps the blood moving really fast while you are
out in the weather. It does no part of one's anatomy
any good to be cold and wet *and still* for long periods.
Not being a doctor, I cannot explain exactly why it
harms one, but that it does do so I can testify, having

35

many times been slack about using waders and having been afflicted in consequence with one of the "worse informities" which Gervase Markham speaks of.

It is difficult to become too warm while wading, but it is singularly easy to become too cold; especially in early spring, when a day's salmon fishing may involve standing for four or five hours in water only a degree or two above freezing-point. Long woollen pants are the first line of defence. Then come woollen socks (two thin pairs are warmer than one thick pair), a pair of really long and thick woollen stockings, and over all a pair of rough flannel trousers. The best stockings I know are those which the Grimsby fishermen use, and which are knitted, I think, in the Faeroe Islands and imported by the Yarmouth stores. They come right up the thigh and are made of raw sheep's wool, which has never been treated in any way and is still full of the natural oil. I have never been able to make up my mind which is the coldest occupation—spring salmon fishing or a night-watch in winter in a small boat. But I have worn those big stockings in boths ituations and can certify that at least my feet were warm.

The purposes of wading are to get within casting range of the fish, or to get clearance from obstacles in the rear such as trees or a high bank which interfere with casting. As I have mentioned in a previous chapter, wading disturbs salmon. It is quite easy, by wading too close, to put a salmon out of its lie, and once it has been shifted in this way it is unlikely for some time afterwards to look at a bait. The many recorded instances of salmon, which had previously refused to take, being woken up by the very rudest agencies, such as the falling debris of a rock blast, falling trees, and so on, so that they afterwards took briskly, is not in any way analogous to the wading occasions of a fisherman. In the instances referred to, the disturbances were short and sharp, not persistent like that made by a wading fisherman. Wood mentions catching a salmon within three yards of him whilst wading, but this must be regarded as exceptional, and explained either by the approach being very quiet or by its being masked by peculiar conditions of light and water. A fish lying in rough water is less easily disturbed than one lying in still water, because the broken surface of the rough water scatters the fisherman's image and the noise masks the scrape of his brogues. But there is no doubt that as a general rule wading does disturb salmon. It is best to do all the casting one can from the bank and then to wade as carefully and quietly as possible, and only as far as is absolutely necessary. Wading, however, is less disturbing than a boat.

Looking after oneself in the water is of course mainly a matter of common sense, but to a fisherman who has never waded in deep water before certain rules may be of help. The first is to fish only when standing still. Do not move whilst fishing out a cast, unless you are sure of the bottom, for a foot moved without care where it is put down may go over the edge of a terrace, or on to a sloping slab, or into a hole or a cleft between two boulders. For the same reason it is wise always to get out of the water by a known route as soon as possible after hooking the fish, unless one can make certain of killing it without moving—a fairly rare contingency. Both these rules apply even when the bottom can be seen perfectly clearly. Being able to see the pitfalls does not help if one is looking at something else. Wading and fishing, as someone has shortly said, deserve separate and exclusive attention.

Where the water is too deep or broken or coloured to enable the bottom to be seen clearly, the need for care is, of course, greater. It is in this situation that a staff is of such immense help, not only as a support, but because it enables the fisherman to test the ground ahead *without moving his feet*. The feet cannot be used for exploring purposes if there is an appreciable current, for it is safe then only to move a foot quickly and transfer weight to it at once. If moved tentatively it would be swept away and its owner thrown off balance.

A staff is an infallible warning of pitfalls, when the bottom cannot be seen. But if for any reason a staff is

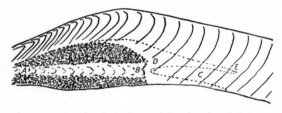

Showing how a whaleback is formed by floods. *DE* is a submerged whaleback at the downstream end of a shingle bank. In high water the shingle bank is covered and there is a strong stream from *A* to *B* which makes a deep scour at *C*. The water over the whaleback is shallow, but the scour *C* is too deep for wading.

not carried and the river is not known, a good rule is to return always in one's own tracks. It is easy, when fishing a pool and wading down a course parallel to the bank, to forget that the ground one has traversed may be simply a whaleback with shallow water on the top and a deep scour between it and the bank. A whaleback is a very common formation and usually consists of a narrow pit of shingle extending at a slight angle downstream from a point near the head of the pool. An attempt to take the shortest route ashore would bring one into the deep scour between the spit and the bank.

Strong water is even more deceptive than thick water; for it not only blurs the bottom but exerts an incalculable pressure against the fisherman's legs. It is impossible to give an accurate rule as to what depth or speed is safe to cross, both because it is difficult to estimate the speed of water merely by looking at it and because so much depends on the quality of the foothold; but from my own experience I should say that, even if the ground is good and a staff is used, a foot of really strong water—going at, say, twelve miles an hour —is as much as anyone can cross without being swept away.

There is only one way to cross fast water. Stand with your back to the current, feet well apart, and lean on the staff, which is propped downstream in front of you. Then edge across, sideways. Do not try to explore with the staff. In this situation it is needed to maintain balance. Place it in front and downstream of the outside foot, transfer most of the weight to the staff and to the inside foot, and you can then wriggle the outside foot across, toe and heel, until it has found a secure hold. Keep as much weight on it as possible while doing this. Then follow up with the inside foot, and you are ready to shift the staff again. The advantage of standing back to the current and leaning forward on to the staff is that when weight is partly taken off a foot in order to shift it, the current tends to force that foot into the ground and not away from it, as would happen if one adopted any other position. The essential thing in fast water is to take as little weight off either foot as possible.

Balance is more precarious in deep water even than it is in strong. When half the volume of one's body is immersed, the weight on one's feet is less than half what it is on dry land. In addition to which, one becomes top-heavy, the centre of thrust being below the centre of gravity. In this situation, balance becomes

more important than firmness of stance, but it is extraordinary how the current itself can be used to maintain
it. If a stumble occurs, it is quite simple to avoid being
upset by executing a sort of jump towards the current
and against the weight of water, lifting both feet and
planting them again lower down. Often in a back-
water, where a considerable swell is coming in from
the surges beyond, one finds oneself fishing practically
on tiptoe, moving one's feet constantly as the current
sweeps this way and that. It all feels extraordinarily
safe, provided one knows the bottom! If one does not,
I need hardly say that nothing feels more dangerous.

The rule that one should make for the bank as soon
as a fish is hooked applies especially to deep wading.
Not only is it impossible to follow a fish through deep
water; it is also extremely easy to be upset by the pull
of the line. A 2-lb. pull at the top of a 15-foot rod is a
30-lb. pull at the butt.

A rise in the water of the lower reaches of a salmon
river often begins without much warning, since the rain
which causes it is generally confined to the hills near
the source a good many miles away. It does not do to
get caught by it. The general look of the weather will
give some idea whether rain is falling inland. If it is
suspected, a rise in the river should be watched for.
In a place where the water is perfectly flat and still, a
swelling of the surface film against the stones will indicate a rise; but a sure and urgent signal to the fisherman
to get out of the river at once is the presence in the
current of dry sticks and bits of grass which have been
lifted clear of the margins by the rapidly rising water.

The general character of a river-bed can generally
be guessed from the formation of the banks. Sandstone
usually means ledges and terraces. The most dangerous
sandstone bed I know is that of the Eden at Arma-

thwaite. There was a fatality in the Castle water in Alan Edwards's time, and after that his guests fished on condition that they did not wade but used the boats instead. The bottom extends flat and level for some distance and then drops sheer into 20 feet of water, with nothing on the surface to indicate the change, the current being quite gentle.

A pool, the banks of which show an outcrop of shale or slate, often has a bed of slippery slabs which slope outwards like the tiles on a roof. Patches of soft clay sometimes occur in shaly river-beds. I once left my brogues in one in the Irfon during a flood, and was lucky that I did not leave myself there as well. It was a horrible place.

A granite-bedded river like the Dart is usually full of rounded boulders and deep holes which as a rule are fairly obvious. The thing to guard against here is getting one's foot jammed in a crack between two boulders. It is a thing that may very easily happen, especially when crossing fast water and you do not realise that your foot is stuck until you try to lift it clear.

Shingle banks are sometimes unsafe. They are apt to start collapsing under one's feet and it may be difficult to get back. Do not trust a shingle bank that slopes at all steeply.

Balfour-Kinnear, in *Flying Salmon*, mentions a danger so horrible that it scarcely bears thinking about— barbed wire lying on the bottom and catching in your wading socks as you walk into it, locking both feet together. It is the sort of thing that might easily happen, for there must be many tons of barbed wire lying in the rivers of the British Isles. If it does, he suggests taking out a penknife and sitting down, under water if necessary, in order to cut the socks away. It is certainly the only remedy, but if one fails to achieve it inside a

minute and a half it seems the only thing left is to try
and drown like a gentleman.

When the worst happens and one takes the one step
too many and is swept away, one should keep on one's
back, one's head upstream, and edge over towards the
bank, aiming at making a landing well downstream.
The reason for keeping on one's back is that it is easier
in that position than in any other to keep nose and
mouth out of water, and the reason for getting one's
head upstream as soon as possible is that one can then
look downstream and decide where to aim for. It is
generally impossible to make headway against the current. At the same time it may be important, owing to
the presence of rapids a short distance below, to make
as little leeway as possible. One should try to edge
across while being swept down, rather in the manner
of a salmon fly.

There is a good old Irish prescription for bringing
warmth into feet which are both soaked and cold. It
applies more particularly to the man who has a long
drive home after standing all day shooting "wid his
two feet in a bog", and it dates from the days when
whisky was three and sixpence a bottle. But I give it
in case it may save a fisherman a cold while he is getting another fish, even if it does cost him three or four
shillings. It is simply this: to take off stockings and
socks and wring them as dry as possible; then soak the
feet of them thoroughly in whisky and put them on
again. The whisky will keep your feet warm for another
hour even though you are standing still.

I should have thought that the old bogey of the peril
of wearing a tight belt outside waders would have been
pretty well laid by this time, but apparently it still
stalks through the pages of angling literature. If I now
attempt to lay it once and for all, I shall immediately

be asked: "Have you yourself ever dived into deep water, wearing long waders with a tight belt outside them?" To that the answer is, "No". But before starting to reason about the matter, I should like to quote from a letter published in the *Field* of 7th September, 1867, by John Lloyd, Jr.: "I put on my wading trousers reeving the string at top as usual round my waist, and dived head foremost into deep water. The result agreeably surprised me, for I found that my legs were gently buoyed up in a horizontal position near the surface of the water, while my head was well above it, and I could use my arms freely in swimming. I swam with the greatest ease for about fifty yards, and it was not for several minutes, and until the water had found its way between the reeving string and my body into the trousers, that I felt any inconvenience from having them on. My legs then began to get heavy, and more depressed in the water, but not so as to prevent my swimming easily."

A. H. Chaytor was another experimenter, and, in *Letters to a Salmon Fisher's Sons*, he gives this opinion: "Many anglers assert that if you do use a belt and do not allow the water to get freely into your waders, if you should have to swim for your life the buoyancy of your legs will drown you by causing your head to go under water and your feet to bob about on the surface like corks. I have tried it more than once by deliberately upsetting out of a boat when crossing the river in my waders, and the result is nothing of the sort. The buoyance is enough to keep your legs still up, but it does not bother you at all, and you swim quite easily, although the clumsiness of the waders makes you very slow, and the weight of water in the waders makes it difficult to get out if the bank is high."

If any argument is needed in support of this evidence, it is, first, that the spare space in one's waders from the knee down is far too small to contain sufficient air to float one's feet high enough to depress one's head; and secondly, that any air imprisoned in the much larger space between one's belt and one's knees is too near the centre of gravity to do so—on the contrary, it is near enough to the centre of gravity to support one's whole body on an approximately even keel. Finally, if one is standing in water which reaches to within 3 or 4 inches of one's belt when the slip occurs, *the waders contain practically no air at all*, because the pressure of the water has driven it out, and even if one is standing in water shallower than this, the pressure drives out a good deal of the air as one falls. I do not believe that one has anything to fear in wearing a belt outside waders, and I should unhesitatingly do so myself if I saw any object in wearing a belt at all.

Drying and storing waders is something of a problem, for dampness rots the twill and heat rots the rubber with which the twill is mixed. It is best to dry them, if possible, in the open air. I do not believe in turning the feet of waders inside out any more than is necessary. They can be turned inside out as far as the ankles quite easily and safely, and if the ankles are then propped open this should be enough to allow the inside of the feet to dry. If for any reason it is impossible to dry them out of doors, they should be placed in a warm room in the house, but not in a drying cupboard or near a fire. Waders are best stored by being hung up in some place that is both cool and dry. They should never be rolled or folded up, for they become stiff when left unused for any length of time and will be liable to crack when undone again.

Worn places in waders should be patched, before they start leaking, with a rubber solution and a patch made of *thin* rubber or cut from an old pair of waders.

CHAPTER V

SUNK FLY—GEAR

And he scanned his fishing-tackle
And his hooks with care inspected;
Put the tackle in his pocket,
And the barbed hooks in his wallet.
                VÄINÄMOÏNEN's *Fishing*: Kalevala, Runo V

A CERTAIN Lord Justice, when asked what were the
three most important characteristics of a successful
barrister, is said to have replied: "The first is animal
spirits; the second is animal spirits; and the third is—
animal spirits". To have said simply "animal spirits"
would have been to give a shorter, but I suppose a less
categorical and emphatic, answer. However, in the
hope that sufficient emphasis will have been achieved
already by comparison with this rather dubious story,
I propose to put the most important characteristic of
sunk-fly gear into one word: proportion. Perfectly pro-
portioned gear means not only delight, but efficiency.
Ill-proportioned gear is both a misery and a disaster.

The factor that regulates the proportion of the whole
outfit is the size of the fly. It has come to be recog-
nised by tackle-makers that the manufacture of fishing
tackle for a particular purpose is as exact a problem in
mechanics as the making of a shotgun or a rifle. Most
fishermen realise this, too, but it is fatally easy to forget
it on going into a tackle-maker's shop to choose an
outfit. Naturally the rods are the first part of the array
to catch the eye. To get one set up, to wave it about

5   45

in that nice high space in the shop that the makers thoughtfully provide, and to say, "Yes, I'll have that one", are all done, nine times out of ten, without considering carefully enough that the sole purpose of a rod is to throw the fly.

The chief mistake that used to be made in choosing a rod was to think that a big rod was necessary to land big fish. Greased-line and thread-line practice has dispelled that idea. The strength of an outfit need only be sufficient to keep a strain on the fish that it can feel and to draw it towards the bank when it is exhausted. The strength of a normal sunk-fly salmon outfit is about four times this requirement. The purpose of all this extra strength is to throw the fly.

Further, it used to be supposed that more or less any well-made and well-balanced salmon-fly rod, no matter what its length and weight might be, would throw any salmon fly properly. But experience has shown that this rough-and-ready approximation is not good enough. Salmon flies vary immensely in weight. A single rod will throw any fly after a fashion, but it will throw properly only a narrow range of sizes suitable to its strength. The sensible course, therefore, is to decide first what flies will be needed and then to choose an outfit which will cast them properly.

Size in a salmon fly is far more important than pattern, and visibility can be only part of the reason why this should be so. One would think that a change in visibility would be satisfied by a change of pattern equally as by a change of size; yet it is the change of size which more often does the trick.

The largest size of hook on which salmon flies are normally dressed is No. 10/0, which measures $3\frac{1}{4}$ inches from neck to bend. No. 6/0, $2\frac{1}{4}$ inches, is about the largest size one needs in this country. From No. 10/0 to No. 5/o the interval between each size of hook is a quarter of an inch. From No. 5/o to No. 3 the interval is an eighth of an inch. A No. 3 hook is an inch long, and is about the smallest size that is fished with a sunk line. When the water is clear and low enough to demand a fly smaller than No. 3, a sunk line will probably not be much good. It is time then to fish in some other way.

In many ways it is a pity that the vast range of patterns which formerly gave a fisherman so furiously to think and the tackle-maker so cunningly to devise, has been shown by experience to be largely unnecessary. The modern salmon fly is a skimpier, less artistic affair, often lacking a "butt", a "cheek", or a "tag", and before long many of the old dressings will have disappeared. Three or four patterns are now generally found to be enough—a dark pattern, like the Beauly Snow Fly or the Purple King, a representative medium blend like the Jock Scott, and a very light silver pattern such as the Wilkinson or the Silver Doctor. In my opinion one ought to acquire a full range of sizes from No. 6/o to No. 3 inclusive in each pattern. Thirty salmon flies may seem a tall order, but the cost of the fishing itself justifies it. Salmon fishing is a sport in which it does not pay to skimp one's gear. Home-tied flies will, of course, cost about a third of what one pays for "boughten" ones.

Weight of wire in the hooks of sunk flies, far beyond the amount required for strength, does not matter in the least. In fact it is an advantage, because it helps the fisherman to do that often difficult thing: sink his fly to the bottom of the river. But the weight should be in the right place—the bend of the hook—not near the point or barb. The point and barb of the hook should be fine, rather than thick, and as sharp as needles.

Never tolerate a blunt or clumsy point for one moment. The safest course is to have nothing whatever to do with it; the alternative is to sharpen it carefully before starting to fish. Do not rub away at the point itself; hollow-grind it by cutting away the metal inside it.

A box of some kind will be needed to carry the flies in. The usual type used for salmon flies is a flat box of aluminium or japanned tin, fitted with rows of metal clips, under which the flies are hooked. The usual type of clip is simply a thin springy metal strip, kinked to take the bend of the hook.

The chief disadvantage of this type is that the flies are not held firmly enough. They wobble about in the clips and lie over the wrong way, so that often the feathers become pinched and tangled and the barbs and points of the hooks blunted or broken. There is one clip on the market fitted with a housing for the point of the hook which keeps the fly steady, but it is still open to the objection that the spring is apt to weaken in course of time and let the hook slip out. Considerable force is required to push a fly under any type of clip and to pull it out again, which is good neither for the clip nor for the dressing of the fly. This trouble can be reduced by keeping the clips oiled.

Of various other kinds of boxes some are fitted with chenille-covered bars, some with pads of porous rubber, like that of which rubber sponges are made, and others simply with pads of soft felt. A salmon fly, however, is a heavy thing and it will not stay put, as a trout fly will, simply by being hooked into some soft substance. Hooking it into something is a bad method of carrying a fly anyway. A hook should never be pulled into anything but a fish.

I am glad to see that in recent years fly boxes made

on the compartment principle are being offered for salmon as well as for trout flies. A salmon fly is very flat and the compartments need not be so deep, though some should be longer than are usually included, to take the big sizes. A recent innovation is a box with magnetic bars. I have not used it, but it sounds an excellent idea.

After the day's fishing, the fly-box should be left open in a warm room so that the flies can dry, otherwise the dampness in the dressings of used flies will rust both hooks and clips in a very short time.

Fly casts have graduated from the carefully-chosen hairs from the tail of a stallion, through silkworm gut, which held the stage for more than a century, to nylon. The object of having a cast, or "leader" as it is often called, is to provide a connection between line and fly which shall be as inconspicuous as possible, and which shall, at the same time, be strong enough to stand the pull of the rod, and springy enough, even when wet, to transmit to the fly the impetus sent along the rod and line in casting.

For these purposes nylon has many advantages over gut, the chief of which are that it does not crack when dry and so need not be soaked before knotting; that its cross-section and consequently its strength, is perfectly even; that it is stronger, size for size, than gut; and that it can be made in unlimited lengths. It is even more elastic than gut, and it does not glitter, as gut does.

Nylon is commonly designated by its breaking strain in pounds or kilos. Sometimes the diameter, either in decimals of an inch or in decimals of a millimetre, is also given. This is quite clear; but the old trade scale for silkworm gut ran from 9X to 0/5 and was sometimes related to the numbers 42 to 25 of the British Standard

Wire Gauge. Since silkworm gut held the field for so long and is still used by some people who prefer it to nylon, these older measurements crop up constantly in fishing literature. To avoid difficulty in comparison, I have set out the various scales in the Appendix. It is interesting to note the improvement in strength of nylon over silkworm gut, particularly as the thickness increases.

The knots that follow were designed for silkworm gut, but I have found them perfectly adequate for nylon as it is supplied at present. When nylon "gut" was first marketed it was a great deal more slippery than it is now—so much so, that many of the standard gut knots were useless, and that great surgeon and fisherman, Dr Stanley Barnes, came to the rescue by devising and most beautifully describing and drawing a whole new series in his book *Knots in Nylon*. For absolute safety these are unsurpassed; and I well remember the delight and relief with which, on receiving from him a copy of his book, I set about practising his ingenious solutions to the problems of making nylon "stick". But for Stanley Barnes's book, the acceptance of nylon by fishermen might well have been delayed. However, the very defect which prompted his research resulted, before many years were out, in a much more stable product, and—perhaps from sheer laziness—I found myself gradually reverting to the older and simpler knots and discovering that, once more, they would do.

The best knot that has ever been devised for joining strands of gut is the famous blood knot. This was first published widely by A. H. Chaytor in 1910, in the first edition of his *Letters to a Salmon Fisher's Sons*, where he recounts how the secret of the knot was revealed to him by a Scottish engineer from Tweedside, who had gone to the length of cutting sections of it and examining them under a microscope in order to see how it was tied. It is not known who the inventor was—possibly some Tweedside fisherman; but the finished knot is so neat that it gives no indication how it is tied.

BLOOD KNOT: WRONG WAY

The turns are placed in the ends while the knot is still in the loose. If the knot is formed like this it is difficult to draw these turns properly tight.

There is a right way and a wrong way of tying it, both impossible to describe on paper but both shown, I hope, sufficiently clearly in the diagrams to be easily grasped. The wrong method produces in the loose a much closer

BLOOD KNOT: RIGHT WAY

The turns are placed in the standing parts. When the knot is drawn tight, these turns transfer themselves into the outer bights and tighten in doing so.

approximation to the finished knot, the turns being in the outside parts, as they are in the finished knot, but in order to draw it tight the ends have to be pulled much harder than the main strands. If the main strands

51

are pulled harder than the ends—which is, of course, the easiest way to tighten the knot—the inner turns of the knot will not be drawn tight.

In the correct (and original) method, the turns are laid at first in the inside parts. But then, when the ends have been drawn gently tight, the heavy pull, which is applied to the main strands, *transfers these turns into the outside parts*, and the enforced lengthening of these parts, which results from this, draws all the turns up solidly tight.

THE BLOOD KNOT DRAWN TIGHT

It needs care and a good light to tie a blood knot properly. For an emergency joint beside the river, when one's fingers are cold or it is not easy to see clearly, the fisherman's knot, single or double, is both simple and safe. It is formed by making a single or double overhand knot with the end of the first piece round the

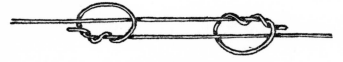

DOUBLE FISHERMAN

standing part of the second, and then doing the same thing with the end of the second piece round the standing part of the first. Pull the overhand knots tight first, round the respective standing parts, and then take hold of the standing parts and pull both knots up together.

Both the blood knot and the fisherman's knot follow perfectly the cushioning principle that should underlie all knots made in gut. Nylon, like gut, is a spongy substance and any tight nip reduces or deforms its section and consequently weakens it. The pull should be distributed as much as possible and sharp turns avoided. It is for this reason that the old-fashioned loop knot for the loop at the upper end of the cast, to which the line is attached, is so sound and strong. On being drawn tight it at first leaves the loop at rather an angle to the

SIMPLE OVERHAND LOOP KNOT

cast, but a little pulling and working with a finger in the loop will soon align the loop properly. The traditional cast-maker's loop knot is the blood loop, which has nothing to do with the blood knot, but which preserves an equally fine cushioning effect. The detail of the turns is shown in the diagram.

For attaching gut to the metal eye of the fly the two

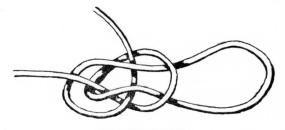

BLOOD LOOP

best knots are the Cairnton knot and the Turle knot. Both are shown in the diagrams. For soundness and simplicity there is little to choose between them. Both grip the hook properly, and there is no dangerous nip anywhere. The Turle knot is perhaps slightly the easier of the two to tie, while in the Cairnton knot the end of

53

the gut is disposed of rather more neatly, pointing down the shank of the hook. Never tie gut to the eye of a hook with a plain slip knot. All the strain falls on the single part of the gut, where it passes under the metal eye. The gut at that point becomes quite flattened by

DOUBLE CAIRNTON

the strain and by the sharpness of the turn, and is constantly being chafed by the eye, as in this position it can exert no grip on the hook whatever. All knots for hooks should be designed to give the gut a good grip of the shank.

One more knot completes all that the fly fisherman need know about this part of his business. It is the

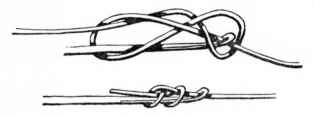

SINGLE CAIRNTON

simple turn called the sheet bend, which is used for attaching the end of the line to the loop of the cast. This bend is commonly used at sea as the quickest certain method of attaching the end of a "sheet", or rope, to the cringle, or eye, in the clew of a sail. Simply pass the end of the line through the loop, round the back of the loop, and across the front of the loop under

54

its own part. There is no need to make an overhand knot in the end of the reel line to stop slipping, for the sheet bend constitutes a perfect jam and will never slip.

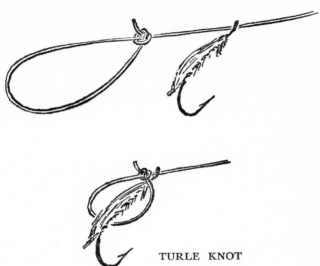

TURLE KNOT

But it is advisable when tying it to leave a quarter of an inch of line spare, to make sure that the jam remains properly formed. This bend has the advantage of being

SHEET BEND

simple to make, safe, and perfectly easy to untie. A Cairnton also does quite well here and allows the end to be tucked away rather more neatly.

One very rarely sees a fisherman in this country use a cast more than 9 feet long in fishing a sunk fly. More often it is only 6 feet. American and Canadian fishermen, on the other hand, consider a cast of between 14 and 20 feet essential. One would, I am sure, do well to follow their example. The heavy line should be kept as far away from the fish as is consistent with proper casting. In coloured water it may not greatly matter if a cast is short; but in clear water there is no doubt that a sight of the line distracts the fish. Like the fisherman that wades too close it may not actually frighten the fish but it certainly disturbs them and makes them bored or sulky. The mere fact that a transparent cast is used at all, and has been used for years, confirms this theory, and if we are going to adopt a principle at all, we may as well do so whole-heartedly and use a cast long enough really to keep the line out of the fish's vision. To do this in deepish water the cast should at any rate be as long as the rod.

A partly tapered cast goes into the wind better than a level one, but the taper should be shorter and steeper than that in a trout cast. Three yards of level gut followed by 2 yards of tapered gut works as well as anything in casting to windward. For casting down wind the taper can be much longer. The size of the gut, like the size for other parts of the outfit, will depend on the size of fly which is to be used. Here the important principle of keeping everything as fine as possible must give way to the even more important principle of keeping everything in proportion. The last link should be just so thick as to hold the weight of the fly firmly without any danger of knuckling at the neck of the fly. A good test is to take hold of the gut an inch above the fly and hold it in a horizontal position. If the fly droops badly, the gut is too thin. 25/100 (0·25 mm.) gut will hold a No. 1 fly quite firmly, but to hold a No. 6/0 fly safely requires 43/100 or 45/100 gut.

The size and weight of the fly determines the size and

weight of the rod, reel, and line. The purpose of the rod, reel, and line is simply to throw the fly, and they should be regarded as auxiliary pieces of gear, entirely subservient to this end.

The rod and line can be considered as a single unit, the purpose of which is to transmit to the fly the force imparted by the muscles of the fisherman. The object

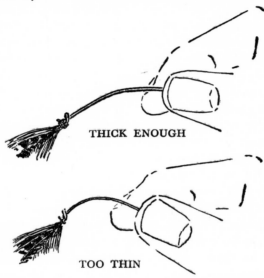

THICK ENOUGH

TOO THIN

of a rod, like that of a bow, is simply to convert strength into speed—strength at the butt into speed at the tip— and it can only do this if the line is of exactly the right weight to suit it. The line must be heavy enough to make the rod bend, yet not so heavy as to stop it springing straight again fast enough to throw the line smoothly and strongly in the direction of the stroke. When the rod is straightening, the tip should travel through several feet at a speed of about ninety miles an hour. If the fisherman could make his own arm do this, there would be no need of a rod at all, as far as casting

57

was concerned. He could throw the line and fly by hand without its aid. The purpose of a rod in casting is to store up momentarily the energy imparted relatively slowly by the fisherman, and then to release this energy practically instantaneously. The first part of this work it does by bending, the second part by springing straight.

Now a line that is too light will not make the rod bend sufficiently to store the full amount of energy imparted to it. The tip will start moving before the rod is fully bent and so will not travel quickly enough to extend the line properly. This can easily be understood by trying to extend even 10 yards of thin string with a stout bean pole. It simply cannot be done. The string will not make the pole bend, and so it is a physical impossibility to get any "zip" into it. The pole can only be waved, not "sprung", and the string will simply fall about in coils.

On the other hand, a line that is too heavy will delay the tip of the rod. It will make the rod bend fully but will not let the tip return again at its maximum speed. This effect of a too-heavy line can be illustrated by lifting two weights with a salmon rod—one of, say, 2 oz., the other of 1 lb. The 2 oz. weight can be flipped up quickly into the air. In lifting the 1 lb. weight the rod will bend almost double before the weight will move; then it will come up only quite slowly.

So much for line and rod, in so far as they relate to each other. Each must exactly suit the other, if such force as the fisherman puts into the butt of the rod is to be transmitted in the proper way to the tip. Now, having seen that the rod and line must be treated as one, we can consider how they are to be related to the fly.

In the first place, a large fly needs a heavier line to

carry it out than a small fly, both because it is heavier and because it offers more resistance to the air. A stronger rod is required to throw this heavier line, for the reasons already discussed. Thus, the size of the fly directly determines both the weight of the line and the strength of the rod.

In my opinion the difference in size between a No. 6/o fly and a No. 3 fly is great enough to make at least two lines essential. It is just possible to cast a No. 6/o fly with a rod that will cast a No. 3 fly. One rod and line can, at a pinch, be made to cast both sizes. But such a rod and line will only cast comfortably the intermediate sizes, say Nos. 3/o to 1. The very large fly can only be cast clumsily and with undue effort, the line not having sufficient momentum to carry it out; while the very small fly flicks like a whip-lash, is difficult to put down gently, and is apt to crack off. It is, therefore, best to have two separate outfits, one heavy, capable of dealing with flies from No. 6/o to No. 1/o, the other light, capable of throwing flies from No. 3/o to No. 3, the strengths of the outfits being so chosen that the overlap indicated will be comfortably within the scope of each rod.

The lines should be double-tapered, *i.e.* thick in the middle, and of an equal thinness at each end, or "forward-tapered", that is, thick in the middle, and with the outer end slightly less thin than the inner. Some experienced fishermen maintain that a single taper—thick at the inner end, tapering to thin at the cast—will throw a fly better; but in my view the laws of mechanics are against them—at any rate for long casting, when most of the dressed line is clear of the reel.

There are many fishermen who have used all their lives a silk line, waterproofed by means of an oil dressing. Very good lines they were, and still are. But research and new materials have been applied to lines, as they have to everything else, and it is in applications from the vast field generically called "plastics" that definite improvements have, here and there, been made. We have plastic dressings, plastic lines with air bubbles in them that float without being greased, hollow, round-braided lines, with a central core, and lines of dense plastic that sink of their own weight.

For sunk-fly fishing we want a line that sinks. Whether to use a silk line or a plastic one is still a matter of taste; but it seems likely that before long silk will disappear, for the fact is that with plastics you can ultimately arrive—not, of course, without mistakes on the way—at any result you aim for. A good plastic line from a reliable maker is already stronger than silk, weight for weight; it can be designed more exactly to fit a particular purpose; and—although time has yet to prove this—it will probably last longer.

Lines, like gut, have at last been endowed with definite classifications for size and weight. The importance of this can hardly be over-emphasised, since it enables that vital factor, proportion, to be achieved for any required outfit, directly from the catalogue, instead of having to be painfully worked out or determined by trial and error. I have set out these classifications in the Appendix.

The line for the heavier of our two outfits will be about ·03 of an inch at the points and ·06 at the centre. The lighter line should be about ·03 of an inch at the points and ·05 of an inch at the centre. The weight numbers will be about #10 and #7.

Double-tapered fly lines are made, as a rule, 35 yards long, since their main purpose—to provide momentum for the fly—is concerned with the actual cast, and 35 yards is about the limit of this. To play the fish, allowing a safe margin for contingencies, another 120 yards of line is needed. This is called "backing", and, since it plays no part in casting the fly but simply provides a connection between the fish and the fisherman, it can be a level line, and may be of undressed silk or flax, or of braided terylene or dacron: but thin, consistent with sufficient strength, so as to occupy as little space on the reel as possible. It should be spliced to the reel line, the splice being made by fraying the end of each line with a penknife, pulling it several times through a piece of cobbler's wax, then laying both ends together so that they overlap about 2 inches, and binding them tightly together with well-waxed thread.

It may not be out of place here to offer a timely warning about the strength of backing. Its breaking strain should be a few pounds more than that of the link of gut nearest the fly. This, in a tapered cast, will be the weakest link, but gut as heavy as that which has to be used with a big fly is surprisingly strong, and the backing for the heavy outfit should have a breaking strain of at least 15 lb. The reason, of course, is that if a fish takes out all the line and something is going to break, it had better be the last link of the cast than some part of the backing. The tapered line will not break, since, being of the heavy gauge necessary to throw the fly, it is generally much stronger than either cast or backing. If the gut breaks, the loss will be only the fly; if the backing breaks, it will be fly, cast, the whole of the tapered line, and part of the backing as well. I speak with feeling on this subject, having once suffered this disaster myself, through imagining that the backing need only be strong enough to stand the pull of the rod in playing the fish, and forgetting how strong the cast was and what would happen if the fish got into a rapid and ran all the line out.

It is most important to dry the line immediately after fishing. It should be pulled off the reel and either wound on to a drier or laid in coils on some flat place that is free from dust and disturbance. Not only the dressed line, which has actually been in the water, but also most of the backing should be pulled off and dried. The latter, whether it has been in the water or not, will need drying, as water will have soaked down into it from the coils of the dressed line. Undressed backing should always be most carefully looked after, because, having no dressing, it is much more liable than the tapered line to rot. An oil-dressed line, if always dried carefully and never stored in a hot place, or left out in the sun, is not likely to become tacky. If it ever does, throw it away. It can be made temporarily fit for service again by rubbing it down with talc powder or French chalk, but for a line that has gone badly tacky there is no permanent cure. Plastic lines or dressings do not suffer from this affliction.

I have tried to show, though I am afraid it may have been a tedious process, the interrelation between line and rod, and how, in order to cope properly with the very big range of sizes of fly needed in sunk-fly fishing, two different weights of line are necessary. It only remains to choose rods which will fit these lines.

It is, of course, the "power" of a rod which has to be fitted to the line. The power of a rod, considered as a factor, may be defined roughly as the weight of the pull at the tip multiplied by the speed with which the tip will spring straight when loaded with that weight. In the first edition of this book, nearly thirty years ago, I wrote "It is, in some ways, a pity that rod-makers do not label each rod with its particular power factor, calculated in this way, so that fishermen can know at once what rod will suit a particular weight. As it is, the fisherman has either to accept the rod-maker's estimate as to what rod is suitable or else go and try the rod and line together and base his choice simply on whether the combination feels comfortable or not." Many fishermen must have felt the need of some such classification, for it has since arrived.

The method used is admirably simple. The outer thirty feet of the line is weighed, and is then denoted by what are known as AFTM Standards. These are numbers, prefixed by the sign # and running from #1 to #12. Fly rods are similarly classified; so that a fisherman buying a line and a rod, each bearing the same AFTM number, can be certain that the *weight* of the line and the *power* of the rod are perfectly matched, irrespective of the *size* of the line or the *length* of the rod, or, indeed, of any other considerations. The matching of the primary relationship of weight to power in this simple way leaves the choice of all other factors wide open, without fear of upsetting it.

As to the "action" of a rod—the *way* in which it stores and delivers the power the fisherman puts into it—this is now generally steely rather than sloppy, since it is realised that a rod with a quick, steely action is far the pleasanter and less tiring of the two to fish with. A steely action is produced partly by hardness of wood and quality of workmanship, and partly by bringing the point of balance well down towards the butt of the rod. Never buy a top-heavy rod. It may, like the Castle Connell rods, be as powerful as a rod of different balance, but is an exhausting and unresponsive thing to fish with.

Length in a rod is a characteristic which is chiefly dictated by the necessity of lifting as much line as possible from the water before the *backward* power stroke is made, and of keeping the line clear of the ground

63

while it is extending backwards just before the *forward* power stroke is made. Before momentum can ever be given to the whole of the line, the line must be approximately straight. Before the backward power stroke, the line can be partly straightened by drawing in the slack by hand or by letting the current straighten the line downstream; but there is still the friction of the water to be overcome before the line can be made to move really fast, and to do this the tip must be high enough from the water to lift the line and far enough from the butt to move through a considerable distance. Similarly, before the forward throw, the line must be fully extended behind, and the longer and higher the backward power stroke has been, the less danger is there of the fly touching the ground while the line is extending. These considerations show that reasonable length in a rod is essential. At the same time, the longer a rod is, the more leverage it exerts, and so the more tiring it is to fish with.

In general, one should be prepared to cast up to 30 yards, and to do this comfortably with a heavy line and a large fly one needs a rod at least 15 feet long. I like one of 16 feet better still. The small amount of extra work it involves is, in my opinion, more than counterbalanced by the additional clearance and control that it makes available. Sixteen feet gives all the clearance necessary. In lengths beyond this, the extra leverage of the rod and the extra weight that has to be put into it in order to maintain its strength are not worth any advantage gained.

The lighter line and smaller fly can be cast more easily, since they offer less frictional resistance both to the water and to the air, and, having less weight, are more easily kept clear of the ground behind. To cast them is quite within the compass of a single-handed

64

rod, and in many respects a single-handed rod is an advantage, both because of the greater delicacy of control which it permits by leaving one hand free to look after the line, and also on the score of economy, because it can be used as well for fishing the greased line, a branch of salmon fishing in which a single-handed rod is almost essential. At the same time, the rod should be as long as can conveniently be managed with one hand; that is to say, about 12 feet.

It must be remembered, though, that a light double-hander of 14 feet is a good deal easier to work and will pick up a sunk line better, especially when making long casts. But the choice can be left to considerations of economy and personal preference.

The vast majority of rods for any kind of fly-fishing are still made of split bamboo, commonly called split cane. It is slightly stronger, weight for weight, than greenheart, and infinitely safer, since it practically never breaks under the terrific strains of casting. Some fishermen used to say that greenheart was sweeter to fish with, but I do not think that this is now true. Split-cane rods are made so perfectly in these days that there is little to choose. I must, however, confess an abiding affection for *spliced* greenheart. No other material, except possibly fibreglass, has an action quite so kind, and none other lends itself in the same way to a spliced joint (it should never be ferruled). But I am bound to admit that it is heavier, strength for strength, and it does, now and then, break without apparent reason. If a greenheart rod is decided on, see that it has a close and perfectly straight grain. Better still, if you can find the right log, from a piece of old harbour piling, as I once had the luck to do, there are your greenheart rods for the rest of your life! Fibreglass is now in general use for shorter rods, and very soon it will be perfected in all lengths; but, as yet, it does not quite equal either the power or the strength of split cane in casting a long and heavy fly line.

The most important of the actual fittings of a rod are the ferrules and the rings. For the honesty of the ferrules one has to rely on the honesty of the maker, for there is nothing—except possibly the length and thickness of the binding below them—to indicate whether the ferrules have proper bayonet ends and have been properly fitted. One can, however, test the fit of ferrules and choose among various types. Any pair of ferrules, of whatever type, should be massively made and should fit each other perfectly. It can generally be seen at once whether they fit well—in an expensive rod it can almost be taken for granted that they do. The best type is the plain suction-joint type, that can be pushed home and pulled apart without any twisting. If they fit properly in the first place and are always greased lightly before being set up, they will never move during fishing and never stick when the time comes to take them apart. Wear can be prevented by always being careful when taking the rod down to grip the ferrules as close to the joint as possible, not to twist them when pulling them apart, and to keep stoppers in them to prevent the entry of dust and grit whenever the rod is not actually set up.

Rings should be as large as is consistent with the limitation of weight needed to preserve a proper balance in the rod. Snake rings, whose defect is that they allow the cast loop or any kink in the line to jam in their corners, have largely given way to the much better "bridge" rings, in which this cannot happen. These are large round rings of hardened steel, set in a bridge mounting, and offer surprisingly little resistance to the line. Agate offers more friction to the line than steel, but agate, on account of its exceptional hardness, is usually put into the top ring and into the lowest ring of the butt, since it is here that the wear is greatest. Agate rings should be watched carefully for cracks. Any sharp blow may crack the stone, and if the crack is unnoticed it will speedily skin the dressing off the line and ruin it.

Reel fittings that screw firmly home over the reel plate are safer than those that merely slip over it. Slip-on or universal reel fittings, as they are called, are always liable to come adrift, and nothing is more infuriating than to have one's reel fall out of them, especially in deep water or when playing a fish.

A rubber button screwed into the end of the butt is comfortable when a fish is being played and when, in order to free a hand for the reel, one rests the end of the butt on one's thigh.

The reel, or reels, for there should be one for each rod, are the least important part of the two sunk-line outfits. Their only functions are to hold the line comfortably, to prevent it being overrun, and to provide a slight brake on the fish when it is taking line out. Apart from that, they should be strongly made and be of the proper weight to balance the rod. A diameter of about $4\frac{1}{4}$ inches for the heavy outfit and 4 inches for the light outfit will be found about right. An interchangeable spool for the lighter reel will enable it to be used also for floating-line methods without either changing the line or buying a fresh reel.

In most reels for fly-fishing the check, which stops the drum overrunning the line, used to consist simply of a spring-loaded pawl bearing on a toothed wheel. The toothed-wheel-and-pawl system still obtains, but the inward wind is now much quieter and in some reels it has been made altogether silent. This is a big advantage, both for the fisherman's nerves, and also

67

for the salmon's, since there is no doubt that the vibration from the old heavy check when winding in often needlessly scared a spent fish at the last moment.

A sensitive and instantly-available brake on a salmon fly-reel for checking a fish is still something of a problem, owing to the difficulty of arranging it so that it does not foul the line when casting. The "wedge drag" adjustment in Farlow's Python and Cobra reels is a useful device.

CHAPTER VI

THE MECHANICS OF FLY-CASTING

... while keeping the line alive in the air. ...
G. M. L. LA BRANCHE, writing on "Dry-Fly
Fishing for Salmon", for the Lonsdale Library

THE last chapter, I am afraid, was full of rather long-winded efforts to explain the mechanical principles which underlie the choice of gear for sunk-fly fishing. I propose that before we consider the more interesting business of fishing with it I should first make a clean sweep of the mechanics by setting out, as shortly as I can, the principles which underlie casting. Casting being a purely athletic operation, dependent on mechanical principles, is best explained by itself, and doing so will, moreover, purge the fishing chapter of unseemly interruptions.

Casting is quite easy, but like any other athletic art, from playing polo to riding a bicycle, it can only be acquired by practice. Being an art and not a science, it cannot be learnt out of a book; but a book can perhaps indicate the lines on which the practice ought to proceed.

A beginner, who has never cast a fly before, should practice at first with a line rather too heavy for the rod. There is nothing like this arrangement for learning to make the rod bend against the pull of the line and to make it *fling* the line instead of merely waving it. Fix the reel firmly into the butt fittings, thread the line through all the rings, seeing that it runs clear of the

69

bars of the reel frame, and put on a cast and an old
fly with the point of the hook broken off. A field or
a lawn with 60 yards of clear length can be used for
the initial practice, but once a line can be got out
fairly decently the sooner one moves to the river the
better.

To take, first, the overhead cast, which is the one most
often used. It looks and is simple enough—a slow lifting
of the rod, that is accelerated into a backward flip, a

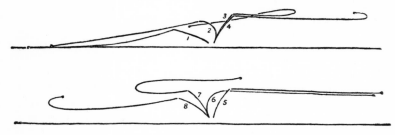

OVERHEAD CAST

1. Line extended with the current. Rod held forward. 2. Backward
drive. 3. Rod springing straight. Line coming back past the fisherman.
4. The pause. Line almost extended backwards. 5. Line fully extended.
6. Forward drive. 7. Rod springing straight. 8. Follow-through.

pause, a flip forward, and a follow-through—but there
is a certain knack in co-ordinating these movements
which is easiest explained and understood if we look
at them separately.

(1) *Straightening and partly lifting the Line.*—Draw 10
yards of line through the top ring of the rod and lay it
out on the grass. Now pick up the rod. There are two
ways of holding a double-handed rod: one, with the
right hand above the reel and the left hand below it;
the other, with the left hand above the reel and the right
hand below it. The former is the most usual and the
better way, because, in casting, the upper arm does
most of the work, and in most people the right arm is

70

the stronger. Most fishermen have the reel handle on the right-hand side, and this is not altogether an advantage because it involves changing the upper grip of the butt from right hand to left whenever it becomes necessary to reel up. If the reel is fitted with the handle to the left and the left hand used for reeling, the right hand need never be moved at all. But, after all, this is simply a matter of convenience. The important thing is to hold the rod and fix the reel in the way which is most comfortable.

The first stage of using the rod to lay the line out in a new direction—in other words, to cast it—is to straighten the line and partly pick it up. If you were actually fishing, the stream would probably straighten the line for you. Suppose, however, that the lawn is a slack pool with no current in it. Lower the rod point, rest the butt against the thigh, and reel up until the line is fairly straight. Then grip the rod again with both hands and hold the line firmly by pressing it against the rod butt with the forefinger of the right hand. Lift the rod, slowly at first to complete the straightening of the line, but at ever-increasing speed until the movement develops into

(2) *The Backward Drive*, sometimes called the "recovery". This is a *violent* jerk backwards and slightly round to the right. It is given mainly by the arm which has the uppermost grip of the rod. There is nothing gentle about it at all. It is a continuance of the upward lift in the sense that there is no pause between the lift and the drive, but it can scarcely be too firm and sudden. Its object is to put as much bend into the rod as possible, without immediately moving the point, so that the rod shall spring straight almost instantaneously and give the line speed enough to come off the water and extend backwards. The backward drive should

begin when the butt of the rod is at about 45 degrees and continue until it is vertical.

(3) *The Pause.*—When the rod is vertical it should be checked, while the line flies back past you, above you, and slightly to your right. Now wait until you feel the line pull against the rod tip—the indication that it is fully extended behind you—and then immediately deliver.

(4) *The Forward Drive.*—This is as violent as the backward drive. Jerk the butt as shortly and sharply as possible from slightly behind the vertical position forward to about 60 degrees, directing the jerk in the direction in which you want the fly to travel.

(5) *The Follow-Through.*—As the line comes forward above you and unrolls ahead of you, follow it through more gently with the rod to about 30 degrees, timing the follow-through so that the rod reaches this angle just before the fly falls on to the water.

I have described the overhead cast in five stages simply for the sake of clearness. In making the cast, the stages are not distinct from one another, except for the slight pause at the end of the backward drive to allow the fly to extend fully behind. The two things to remember in casting are: first, that while the line is in the air the rod must be kept in touch with it, either pulling it or being pulled by it, or else the line will fall to the ground; and second, that it is impossible to break a split-cane salmon rod in casting when using it with its proper weight of line. The sharp jerk of the recovery and of the forward drive can scarcely be too fierce, especially when fishing a long line. Timing a cast, like timing the stroke of a cricket bat, cannot possibly be learnt from a description, but soon comes by practice. The only advice about timing that I think might be useful to a beginner is that the pause between the recovery and the forward drive should be *quite long*.

It is not often that the overhead cast is made with the line held throughout by the forefinger of the right hand, as described above. It is easier to make a long cast by allowing 3 or 4 yards of the line to hang in a loop (floating on the water, if necessary) between the lowest ring and the reel, and using the momentum given to the remainder by the forward drive to draw this line out. This dodge is called "shooting" the line. There is nothing in it, except to time exactly the moment to lift the forefinger of the right hand and let the loose line go. This moment occurs at the end of the forward drive; the instant you feel the rod springing straight, let go.

The overhead cast can be made over either shoulder. If the river is flowing from left to right as regards the fisherman, *i.e.* if he is fishing from the right bank, the current extends the line downstream to the right, and the line is brought back more easily over the right shoulder. Similarly, if the river is flowing from right to left, it is easier to bring the line back over the left shoulder and make a back-handed cast.

Other casts which are useful to the salmon fisherman are the "switch" and the "spey" and, occasionally, the "underhand" cast. The underhand cast needs little describing, for it is simply a modification of the overhead cast, designed to keep the line as low as possible so as to clear overhanging trees. The recovery is made with the rod almost horizontal, yet with the path of its tip forming, in the vertical plane, a slightly humped trajectory, so that the line flies back above it. During the forward drive the tip is still low but is moved slightly upward, and the line goes out very close on itself, or, as fishermen say, with a very "narrow entry". A well-made underhand cast enables 20 yards of line to be sent out with no part of it ever more than 10 feet from the ground.

73

The switch and spey casts were designed to prevent the line going behind the fisherman and so catching in trees or high banks in rear. Both are continuous-motion casts, that is to say, recovery and forward drive merge into one movement, without any pause between, since the line cannot be allowed to extend except in a forward direction. The idea is to give great momentum to a large loop of line, so that it shall pass part of this momentum on to the rest. To make a

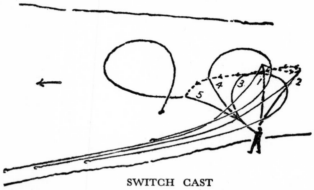

SWITCH CAST

(In this and the succeeding diagram the numbers simply indicate the sequence of the various positions shown.) The dotted line shows the path of the rod point.

switch cast straighten the line, raise the rod slowly until it is slightly beyond the vertical, then chop it forward and downward really hard in the direction the fly is to be thrown. A loop should then travel away in this direction, picking up and relaying the line as it goes. It is because of this rolling loop that the switch cast is sometimes called the rolling cast.

In the cast just described only a part of the line is clear of the water at any one time. In the spey cast the whole of it is clear, and this makes the spey a more efficient cast, though possibly more difficult to do properly. The line

74

being extended downstream, carry the rod point low
and well downstream till it is almost pointing down the
line. Now bring it strongly upstream across your front
and at the same time move it diagonally upwards till
it is extended above and slightly behind your upstream
shoulder, slightly behind the line of the bank, and at
45 degrees to the ground. Without pausing in the least,
cut it hard forwards and downwards in the direction
the fly has to go. The line should all travel, clear of the
water, upstream across your front, follow round the big

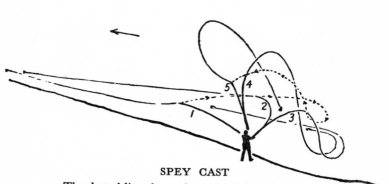

SPEY CAST

The dotted line shows the path of the rod point.

loop that the passage of the rod has made upstream and
in front of you, and so lay itself out in the new direction. To do the spey cast properly one really needs a
top-heavy rod of the Castle Connell type, and a line
heavier than usual. But with practice a fair fist can be
made of it with the usual gear, and it is a most useful
cast to master.

These four casts, the overhead, underhand, switch,
and spey, are all that a salmon fisherman needs for the
purpose of throwing his fly. Shooting the line is in-
dispensable when throwing a long distance and soon

75

becomes so automatic as to be an integral part of both the overhead and underhand casts. In the continuous-motion casts it is much more difficult. Because momentum can be given only to a small part of the line, and because the entry is wider, much more force has to be applied, and little of it can be spared for shooting. But these are emergency casts, and were not designed for throwing a long line.

Apart from actually throwing the fly out to a particular point, it is often of the greatest importance to be able to make the line fall in a particular way. For on the way the line falls will often depend the way the fly moves after it has been thrown, and the movement of the fly in the water must at all times be as much under the control of the fisherman as possible. Suppose, for instance, that there is a good lie on the far side of a fast rush and that the only available stance is immediately opposite it. If a straight line were thrown, it would be caught at once by the current and the fly whirled out of the lie before the salmon had a chance to take it. But, if a slack line is thrown, the current takes an appreciable time to straighten it, and during that time there will be no drag on the fly and it will hang in the lie.

In throwing a slack line, as in all other variations of normal casting, the ordinary overhead cast is the one to use. The underhand cast can be adapted to a few of these special purposes. But, for the reasons previously explained, the continuous-motion casts are not suitable for any of them.

To cast a uniformly slack line with an overhead cast, check the point of the rod immediately the forward drive has been given and raise it to the vertical while the line is unrolling. Then, when the line is almost unrolled and still in the air, lower it quickly. Do not shoot any line.

An even more effective but less tidy way of casting a slack line is to aim high, put far more power into the drive than would be necessary for a normal cast, and shoot only a moderate amount of line. The effect is that the line extends fully in the air before its momentum is exhausted, and bounces back to fall slackly on the water. This method involves a certain amount of risk that the fly may double back and foul the cast.

Slack line can be concentrated near the fly by making an overhead cast and shooting late. Do not shoot till the line is almost unrolled.

It is often useful to be able to throw the line so that it lands with a curve in it. Make an overhead cast, and while the line is being shot flick the tip of the rod strongly round in the direction the middle of the curve is to lie. This throws the shot line over in a curve in that direction. This sounds a difficult cast, but it is surprisingly easy and smooth. The rod naturally bends forward slightly after the power stroke, and instead of easing this bend by following through with the butt, as in the finish of a normal cast, you check the butt at about 45 degrees and use the forward bend of the rod as the beginning of the flick. The beginning of the flick and the lifting of the forefinger from the line about to be shot take place at the same moment. The flick can be made to right or left, according to the direction in which the curve is to lie.

For laying a curl in the gut cast near the fly, at the same time making the line fall straight, the procedure is quite different. The best cast for this is the underhand cast and it should be made on the same side as the curl is to lie. If the curl is to lie upstream, the cast should be made on the fisherman's upstream side, and *vice versa*. Use rather more force than usual and shoot a little line. The effect is this. In the underhand cast the rod in the forward drive is nearly horizontal and the fly, as it goes out, passes beyond the tip of the rod and approximately level with it, the line going out with a narrow and practically horizontal entry. In this case the extra force put into the drive combines with the shooting of a small amount of line to produce a "bounce" when the line is extended above the water, and this flips the fly round so that it falls downstream of the cast. Delay the shoot a little, until the line is almost extended. Use

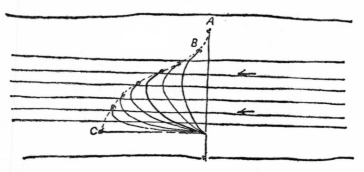

THE EFFECT OF A SQUARE CAST ACROSS FAST WATER

The line is swept into a bow; the fly is dragged out of the ease into which it was cast and skids across the current at much too high a speed.

only a very little more force than is necessary for a normal cast—if too much force is used the bounce becomes too pronounced and makes the whole line spring back and fall slack, as in the cast designed for this purpose.

These various ways of casting are for making the fly move as the fisherman wants it to during the first part of its journey. But the good effects of the cast are only of short duration. Before the fly and line have travelled very far the current will have taken charge. To stop its doing so and to keep the fly still under control, there are various dodges which have come to be known—

perhaps on the analogy of the functions of heel and leg in guiding a horse—as "aids" to casting. Most of them are quite simple, such as following the fly round with the rod point, giving slack line, and so on, and do not require any physical skill. But there is one—the most important—which calls for so much cunning that I think it should be described separately.

It is an apparently simple movement of the rod, designed to pick up the bag of the line which the current

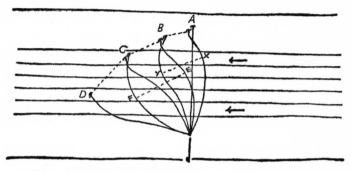

THE EFFECT OF MENDING A SQUARE CAST

The purpose of mending is to give the line further to travel than the fly, so that if the line is in fast water and the fly in slow water, the two will keep pace with each other. The diagram shows the line mended as soon as the cast was made. Thus while the fly was travelling from A to B the line had to travel from X to Y before it could drag the fly. When the fly reaches B, the line is mended again and has to travel from E to F while the fly moves from B to C. A third mend gives the fly time to come round slowly from C to D.

has made and lay it in an upstream curve, without moving the fly. The object of doing this is to keep the fly moving slowly, instead of being dragged swiftly across the current by the bellying line. The movement is called "mending" the line and was developed and brought to the fore by A. H. E. Wood as an essential part of his technique of fishing with a floating line, though references to it in many books show that it was

practised long before his time. It is done simply by a
quiet semicircular movement of the tip of the rod from
a downstream to an upstream direction. And that is
about all the description that it is possible to give. The
rod point is kept rather low, the butt rather high, the
arms are kept rather stiff and are carried forward as
the "roll" is made, so as to reduce drag on the fly, but,

MENDING

(The numbers simply indicate the sequence.) The dotted line shows
the path of the rod point.

apart from these injunctions, all one can say is that
mending is a quiet semicircular movement through a
fairly wide arc.

Wherein a successful mend, which picks up 15 yards
or more of line and rolls it smoothly upstream—one of
the most beautiful sights in the whole of fishing—differs
from dozens of other quiet semicircular movements,
which throw a small ineffectual loop 5 yards from the
rod and jerk the fly a yard or more, is by eye impossible
to distinguish. The secret is best expressed in Wood's
own italics: *the whole movement is quite gentle and slow*.
The slightest hurry or flick will jerk the fly and reduce
the length of line mended. Not only must the movement
be slow—it must also be perfectly timed, the rod point
keeping just ahead of the line and giving it only just
enough lift to turn it over without jerking the fly.

80

CHAPTER VII

SUNK FLY—ORTHODOX AND HETERODOX

After two or three consecutive days of covering the water, one can go on covering it automatically, like walking, and think about one's sins, or compose poetry.
PERCY NOBBS, *Salmon Tactics*

There is a way of taking the belly out of a line, which was taught me by an old fisherman when fishing the Kirkcudbright-shire Dee in my younger days.
MAJOR J. P. TRAHERNE, writing on "Salmon Fishing" for the Badminton Library in 1885

THE traditional way of salmon fishing was almost too simple for words. You waded in at the head of the pool until you could wade no further. You then threw as long a line as you could cast, well downstream and across towards the opposite bank, and let the current swing it slowly round until it was directly below you. You then stepped two paces downstream—never more and never less—and cast again. If you were fishing the Shannon you waggled the rod while the fly was in the water. If you were fishing in Scottish waters, where waggling the rod was frowned on, you did not waggle it, especially if there was a gaunt Highland gillie, who disapproved of waggling, standing hard by with a home-made gaff. In this way you progressed mechanic-ally down the pool, coming to life only in order to play a fish, or to pacify your attendant and fortify your own numbed senses with a dram from the flask.

It was often a dull business, this way of fishing. Probably more salmon have been caught by it than by all our new-fangled methods put together, but probably that is because our new-fangled methods have only been going for such a very short time. It was, however, evolved, consciously or unconsciously, to achieve certain ends, and in order to see what these ends are we shall have to plunge once more into theory.

Whenever the air is appreciably colder than the water, salmon will be disinclined to take a bait near the surface. Cold has this further effect on salmon, as it has on most forms of life: it makes them sluggish. In spring, especially, salmon are curiously torpid. This may be partly due to the feeding instinct being displaced by the spawning urge, but not entirely, for the early springers will take a bait very readily if it is brought close enough in front of their noses. The feeding habit which they acquired in the sea persists for a while; it is the drop in temperature which makes them so reluctant to chase far after a bait. Fishing for them while they are in this condition, therefore, resolves itself into two main concerns—keeping the fly deep in the water, and, in the early months at any rate, making it come as slowly as possible across the fish's view. The whole art and science of sunk-fly fishing is directed to these two ends.

In fishing the sunk fly the fisherman's chief enemy is the current. It does the two things he wants to prevent. It tends to keep the line high in the water, and, by catching the centre of the line and forming a bag in it, it at once drags the fly away from the lie it was cast into, and brings it across any other lie that may be in its path at much too high a speed.

Hence the traditional long line and downstream cast. By this means the line was placed nearly parallel with the current, so that it remained fairly straight and did not get swept into a curve and drag the fly. But, even so, the current still tended to prevent the line from sinking. Because the tip of the rod was above the water and was holding the line against the current, the force of the latter was acting on the lower side of the line and tending to keep it up. Using as long a line as it was possible to cast only reduced this effect; it did not do away with it.

There were further disadvantages in this orthodox way of fishing. The fly, it is true, could be made to cross very slowly in front of the fish, owing to the small lateral pressure exerted on the line by the current; but salmon lie with their heads upstream, and, owing to the fly being held against the current, it was always presented to them end-on—the worst possible position as far as visibility and attractiveness are concerned. Again, the fly was always "on the dangle", as the saying is. In other words, it was, throughout the cast, held hanging by the current at the end of a straight line. This meant that a fish coming up to the fly from below would rarely be hooked in the safest place—the angle of the jaw. More often it would merely be pricked in the nose, and accused of "coming short"; for any "strike" that the fisherman gave would tend to drag the fly out of the fish's mouth instead of pulling it in.

References in many of the earlier books hint that the best fishermen—the men who brought their brains to bear on their sport as well as their muscles—never let themselves be bound by any set method of fishing. The trick of "mending" a line upstream, to take the belly out of it and prevent its dragging the fly, was known and practised at least sixty years ago, and that shows that the men who knew it cast their lines much more squarely across the stream, because mending is unnecessary in a downstream cast. Probably they used also many of the other "aids" for preventing drag, for

7

when the advantage of a thing is made abundantly clear one soon learns how to do it.

But the chief credit for developing the art of preventing drag in fly-fishing for salmon and giving it wide publicity must go to A. H. E. Wood, of Glassel, who brought it almost to perfection whilst working out his method of fishing with a floating line. Thanks to his experiments, sunk-line fishing need not be the monotonous business it once was. The greased-line technique of fly control, applied to sunk-fly fishing, makes every cast a campaign and gives the fisherman an interest in the flow of the water and the movement of his fly which the orthodox method never induced him to take.

It is almost an accident that the technique which Wood found necessary for fishing a floating line should also apply so aptly to fishing with a sunk line. In fishing a floating line prevention of drag is an end in itself. In fishing a sunk line it results in one of the two chief ends which sunk-fly fishing aims at—making the fly sink. If the fly and line are allowed to move at the speed of the water round them, they will sink of their own weight. It is only when the line is held against the current that the current forces it up, makes it sag in the middle, and not only keeps the fly high in the water but drags it round at too great a speed.

Roughly, the tactics in greased-line fishing are to cast across or slightly upstream and to mend, if necessary, throughout the whole cast. Often a mend or a succession of mends is insufficient in fast water to prevent drag. Resort must then be had to the other aids. In sunk-line fishing these are of even greater importance than mending, because the sinking of the line makes it impossible to mend more than once in the same cast. As soon as the line touches the water it can be mended once, but the moment it sinks further mending becomes impossible, and, in order to prevent drag, the other aids must be called into play. These are quite simple and are all directed to preventing the line being held against the current. "Leading" is the simplest, and consists merely in following the line down with the rod point, so as not to let it pull against the rod. In casting a short line, where little force is needed, the follow-through can be dispensed with and the cast finished with the rod point high and upstream, so that a much longer "lead" can be made. Stepping downstream is another means of easing the line down with the current. And giving slack has the same effect.

In addition to the prime advantages of sinking the fly and letting it move slowly, this greased-line technique of the square cast, supported by the aids, carries with it several other advantages which the old method did not possess. For one thing, it presents the fly broadside to the fish, instead of end-on. The fly is not being held pointing upstream at the end of a taut line, but is drifting naturally, more or less square to the current. This provides the fish with a better view of the fly and also facilitates hooking. Again, the greased-line technique, embodying as it does a squarer cast, enables a much shorter line to be used. Finally, it also enables the fly to be thrown into lies which could not be reached from above, as, for instance, when the only stance for casting is opposite the lie or where the lie is guarded on the upstream side by a rock which sticks up out of the water and would foul a line cast from above.

It rather sounds, from this catalogue of advantages, that the greased-line technique applied to sunk-line fishing has completely displaced the old traditional downstream method. Well, it has, for a great many purposes, but the downstream method has special uses which it would be a mistake to overlook. In fishing the downstream way the fly is presented badly, it is often fished too shallow, but it *can* be brought quite slowly over the whole arc of its path. The greased-line technique fishes the fly properly, but, owing to the fact that a sinking line can only be mended once or at most twice, the fly can only be "hung" for a relatively short time. However much the aids are brought into play, it is quite impossible to hang a fly on the far side of a fast rush indefinitely. Sooner or later the intervening line will be caught by the current and will drag the fly away.

The downstream way, then, is the best method for covering the *whole* of a pool in which the lies are unknown. However fast the stream is, the fly can be made to move quite slowly, because it is held from above at the end of a taut line. The greased-line technique is invaluable to the sunk-line fisherman for working particular lies; the old orthodox technique is the best way of fishing unknown, shallow, and featureless water.

Now let us have done with theory and get down to the river. Suppose that it is one of those typical sunk-fly days in early spring, hard and clear, with a bitter cold east wind, the hills still white, the river running full and black. You will need warm clothing today, both above and below the water-line, for the river is well-nigh at freezing point and the air is a degree or two below it.

You have all your gear?—even down to the paper clips and the carborundum? Good. Probably only the heavy outfit will be needed today, as this weather demands big flies and does not look like changing. Set up the rod, fix the reel on firmly and see that you thread the line through *all* the rings of the rod. If one is missed out, the line will probably get hooked up round it. As you will be starting with a big fly, about 5/o, you will

86

need a heavy cast. This can be tied on to the line with the sheet bend described in Chapter V.

The day is hard and clear, but not bright, so we will choose some big dullish-looking fly like a Beauly Snow Fly. The old rule is: bright day, bright fly; dull day, dull fly. This is sound doctrine. I always used to think that it should be the other way round; for it seemed to me that a bright fly would show up better on a dull day, whereas on a bright day a dull fly would be good enough. The fact is that a brightly coloured fly is out of place on a dull day. A salmon presumably thinks that a fly is something alive, and the live things of the stream do not flash and glitter on dull days. Conversely, on a bright day, when everything below water is a mass of moving gleams and shadows, a dull, black-looking object would be quite out of place.

Tie the fly to the end of the cast with a Turle knot or a Cairnton knot, and make sure that the knot is correct before pulling tight.

All ready? Very well, then. Sling the strap of your gaff handle round your shoulder, pick up your rod, and decide where you are going to begin. The pool has a strong surging rush at its head which runs deeply in towards the further bank and eases as the water gets deeper and the pool takes a slight bend. Your own side of the pool is shallow and rippling, with a bed of stones shelving gradually out until they are lost to view in the "broo" just on the edge of the fast water. Just below the bend, an outcrop of rock on the far side of the river constricts the water into a "waist" where, although still deep, it gathers speed considerably. Finally it spreads, moving more slowly, into a broad deep tail where circular crinkly patches on the surface indicate submerged boulders. There are trees on both sides of the pool.

As it is spring, and cold into the bargain, we shall

miss out the fast rush and begin about half-way down
the run where the water is deeper and beginning to
slow up. As we don't know the pool, and the surface
here is moving quite steadily with no mark in it to
indicate a lie, we shall begin by fishing downstream in
the usual way. Wade in well above the place where
your fly is to land, and cast as long a line as you can
downstream at an angle of about thirty degrees to the
flow of the current. It does no harm to mend at once
in order to let the fly sink quickly before starting to
"fish" it. When the line tightens, let it come round as
slowly and as deeply as possible. Don't waggle the rod.
Waggling it from side to side has no effect whatever
on the fly, as the water prevents the "waggle" ever getting to it. The only way to move the fly is to draw it up
in slow jerks, but this is best left until the end of the
cast. When the fly is on the dangle below you, step
down a couple of paces while the fly is still in the water,
and then lift the rod gently and at the same time take
in by hand, in slow jerks. the line which you are going
to shoot at the next cast. Letting the fly down a little
and then fetching it back in this way will often induce
a salmon which has been following the fly round to
take hold at the last moment, and is a good way to
make use of the two steps downstream, which are
necessary, in any case, for covering fresh ground.

Cast again, shooting the line you have gathered in.
Don't wind any line in or take any more off the reel.
You want to cast the same length of line each time,
so as to be sure of covering the whole pool in even
"swathes" in order that every fish in it may have a
chance of seeing the fly, and, moreover, that each fish
shall see the fly before it sees the line. If a fish offers but
does not take, do not forget to step upstream before
casting to it again.

88

Half-way round, the line stops. What is it, a fish or a snag? You have tightened with a good firm pressure, and nothing yields. Work downstream a little, and pull from the side. That will upset his balance if it is a fish, and start him off. Still nothing doing? Must be a snag, then: a rock or a tree. Tear off plenty of slack, and let the current take it down past the place where the fly is hung up. Now give a good jerk. The pull of the current on the bag of the line will make the jerk on the fly come from below. Still it does not come away. Had the fly been merely hooked against a rock the pull of the current from below would have freed it. The hook must be sticking in some old sunken branch.

You don't want to lose a brand-new seven and-six-penny fly, so you manufacture what is known as a "traveller". Find a short stout piece of wood, tie a piece of twine (which you carefully remembered to bring with you!) round the middle of it, and hook a paper-clip on to the twine. Next hook your line into the paper-clip and let the traveller run away down the line. Let it float well below the snag and then jerk good and hard. This should do the trick. It has? Good enough. Have a look at the hook point before you go on fishing, and, if it seems at all dulled, give it a rub with the carborundum.

The water is deepening so that you can't wade? If there were a boat on this pool, we would use that, and try "harling". Harling is simply the orthodox downstream method adapted to fishing from a boat. The fisherman need not cast at all. He simply keeps his rod low, and lets the line and fly trail downstream. The boatman has all the fun. His business is to edge the boat to and fro across the river, head to current, and work the fly with the boat. He must keep the boat moving steadily, and not let it drop downstream until it reaches the end of its traverse. The most likely time in harling is at the end of each traverse, when the boatman lets the boat drop down a couple of yards and starts working it across again in the opposite direction. This makes the fly sink a little, and check, and then start off again rather quickly back across the river—

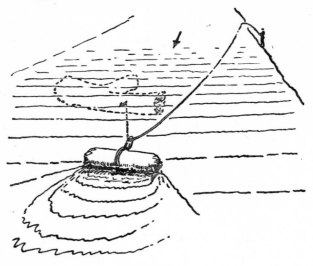

TRAVELLER

behaviour that a salmon which has been following it can seldom resist. But everything depends on the boatman.

As there is no boat here, the only remedy is to alter the angle of cast, so that the fly can be made to reach the "taking" water. Cast square across, and mend up, looking out behind you for trees. . . . Bang! I should have warned you sooner. You were casting well downstream before, so that the line behind you was flying clear over the water. Now the squarer angle has brought it over the bank at your back, and the cast has smashed fair and square into the twigs at the end of that black branch 20 feet above the ground. No, *don't* jerk it! Never try to free a fly from a branch by jerking the line. Drawing it very slowly and gently towards you will very often ease the fly clear; jerking it only makes the fly spin round a twig and fix the cast

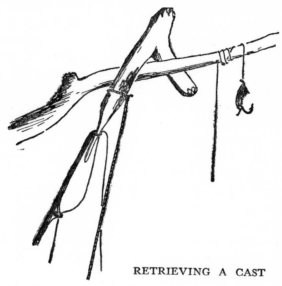

RETRIEVING A CAST

there for good and all. And that is just what has happened now.

You daren't pull the branch down for fear of breaking the gut? Well, there is a remedy for everything in salmon fishing, except failing to catch a fish. Take out the trusty twine again, cut a strong forked stick, and tie an end of the twine to the end of one of the prongs. Pare down an inch or two of the end of that prong until it will slip into the top ring of the rod. Slip it into the ring, lift the forked stick up with the rod, and hook it over the branch. Now you can take hold of the twine and pull the branch down.

Try the switch or the spey cast until you are past that troublesome branch.

At the "waist" of the pool the projecting rock on the far side deflects the water, leaving a quiet ease on the far edge of the current which looks a likely place for a salmon to lie. Up to now you have been searching the good-looking but rather even and featureless lower half of the run with a long downstream line, and practically the only variation you made in your fishing was to make a rather bigger mend and give the fly more time to sink as you came to the deeper water. You were searching the water, then. Now you have a definite place to aim for. What you want to do is to hang the fly for as long as possible in the ease on the far side of the current.

Cast with a good big mend in the line, making your fly fall at the top of the ease, and mend again as soon as the line touches the water. It is most important to get as much of the line as far upstream as possible, so that the fly has plenty of time to sink before the line gets below it and starts dragging it.

Nothing doing there? Let us move down, then, and try the rocks in the tail. Take each likely-looking one in turn, beginning with the nearest. Each lie is a separate problem, just as the ease behind the rock point was. The slowly crinkling patch on the surface gives you a shrewd idea where a salmon is likely to be lying and you are going to aim at that particular lie. Make the fly land slightly beyond and well upstream of the "boil". Mend carefully and use every other aid you can think of to prevent dragging the fly.

Yes, that was a fish all right. No mistaking that gleam under water as he thought better of it and turned back into his lie. The fly interested him and he followed it out for a short way. Try him again at once, sinking the fly even deeper if possible. No result?

Snip off the big fly and put up a fly three sizes smaller. There he is again—a definite pluck this time. But still he won't take.

Cast once more, let the fly hang only a moment in the lie and then pull it away fairly fast. This is called "pulling off". You have already been doing it as the fly came round to the dangle when you were fishing a downstream line in the run, and it often persuades a hesitating fish to dart at the fly. Still no good. Well then, you had better leave this fish for the present. Further casting just now would only put it down for the rest of the day.

We will go back to where we started and fish down again, using the small fly. You need not be afraid of fishing the pool several times. We started with a fly even larger than the weather and water demanded, because a big fly sinks better than a small one, and it is better to change down than to change up. A big fly often wakes salmon up and makes them ready to take a small one afterwards.

You fished down the dub and tried the ease behind the rock point without result, and here you are again opposite the lie of the refractory salmon.

Before trying for him again, have a look at the hook point. You know that the fish is there and "in the humour", and you should not leave anything to chance. Broken off? Well, there is nothing surprising about that. It is the easiest thing in the world for a hook to hit a stone on the back cast, especially when a long line is being cast; and that is what must have happened as you were wading down the run with the shingle behind you. Sometimes the fact advertises itself by a slight click; but, apart from that, you have only your suspicions that you have been casting badly to warn you that you may be fishing with a pointless hook.

Put on a duplicate fly and try the fish from slightly upstream, casting as carefully as possible and taking the greatest care not to drag the fly. Well, what is the matter with this fish? This time he won't even take an interest. Perhaps this smaller fly is not going deep enough, or perhaps the angle is wrong. Move down below him as quietly as possible, and cast upstream to him. An *occasional* upstream cast often pays, as the fly sinks very quickly if cast upstream, there being far less drag. It also alters the angle of the cast and may let a dullish-looking fly catch the light and reveal itself to the fish. The disadvantages of fishing always upstream are that the line may come over the fish before the fly if you don't know exactly where the fish is lying, and that a scared fish, if it moves at all, will run upstream and disturb those not yet fished for.

You think the former of these disadvantages is now being perfectly illustrated? I don't agree. You cast quite correctly, keeping the line well to this side of the lie and the fly just in the near edge of the fish's "window". Probably you are getting fed up. I don't blame you. Here you have fished twice down this excellent-looking pool, you have found a fish that looked like a taker, and you have angled for him very skilfully in a number of different ways. Well, salmon fishing is like that. I know a man—a good fisherman, too—who fished every day for a month on a good beat of a good river, and on the last afternoon of his last day caught one salmon. Including the expenses of his journey and hotel, he estimated that that salmon cost him £150. On the other hand, a single rod has been known to catch thirty-six salmon in a day. As I once heard an old West Country pilot reply in evidence, when asked what would happen in certain circumstances, which counsel set out at great length and with minute exactness: "Well, sir, that's all accordin'!"

But when you think you are beaten, that is the time to fish most carefully. The best fly, as the gillie said, is "the flee that's in the watter". There is one more trick I can think of that is well worth trying. By standing on a rock at the narrowing of the pool opposite the rock point, it is just possible, by casting a long line, to cover the lie from directly above. Cast below and to one side of the lie, let the fly sink, and then draw it steadily up past the fish. You are not in such a hopeless position for hooking the fish as might appear, for if he takes the fly at all he will turn sideways and snatch it.

If you can see the fish, the cast can be made more accurately. You cannot see this one, but the rock boil shows you to within a yard or two where he is. Don't cast too far below him so that he sees the line. If the fly lands a couple of yards below him, that will do. Good! You made the cast perfectly. Now draw. . . . Bang! He's got it, and you are into your first salmon.

CHAPTER VIII

FROM A VIEW TO A DEATH

He, knowing it a Fish of stubborne sway,
Puls up his rod, but soft, (as having skill);
Then all his line he freely yeeldeth him,
Whilst furiously all up and downe doth swimme
Th' insnaired Fish.
                    WILLIAM BROWNE, *Britannia's Pastoral*

A merry fish on a stallion hair,
'Tis a pleasant thing to lead . . .
                    THOMAS TOD STODDART

YOUR fish turned out of his lie and took the fly with a sideways snatch as you were drawing it up past him, stopping the draw of the rod with a good solid jar that went through you like an electric shock and leaves you in no doubt that he is properly hooked.

A salmon, as a rule, takes a fly quite slowly. For a fly, if it is being ordinarily fished, is normally moving quite slowly. It is either hanging at the end of a taut line and sweeping gently sideways, or else it is being given a slack line and drifting quietly down at the same speed as the current. The fierce "rug" that the fisherman sometimes feels when a salmon takes generally means that the fly was moving fast when the salmon took it, either skidding across the current or else being deliberately jerked by the fisherman to induce the fish to take it.

If you had seen the rise, I should have advised you not to strike at once, but to give the fish time to go down with the fly and close his mouth on it. But you should not have waited too long. A fly for sunk-fly fishing is big and heavy, and the fish soon feels the iron and spits it out. You would have tightened steadily and firmly as soon as you saw the curve of the salmon's back as he went down.

If a salmon takes well down out of sight, as usually happens in sunk-fly fishing, tighten as soon as you see the line stop or feel a "rug". The fish has actually taken the fly into his mouth before you see the line stop and you can depend upon it that by the time the line does stop he has got hold properly. Tighten at once, before he feels the big hook and spits it out.

A fish taking a skidding fly usually hooks himself. And the same applies to a fish that takes a fly at the end of a taut line, as when the fly comes to the dangle after a square cast or is being "pulled off" or worked back against the current, as you were working yours when you hooked your fish. Unless he turns sideways at the fly, as your fish did, a fish that takes on the dangle is usually poorly hooked, somewhere in the nose. It is advisable to let him have a slack line at once, get well below him, and then pull hard. With luck the weak hold will give way and the fly will come back into the angle of his jaw and re-hook him securely.

What will probably surprise you about the fish which you have hooked is that if you give him slack line at once, the chances are he will remain perfectly still. Give it him, at any rate, and see. Nine times out of ten a hooked salmon will keep still if given a slack line, and this gives you a chance to get out of the water and below the fish.

It is an extraordinary phenomenon, this inertia of the salmon that is given a slack line. It may be due simply to bewilderment, but it looks like complete indifference, for a hooked salmon will keep still almost

97

indefinitely if there is no pull on the line. It would be interesting to see if a hooked salmon would take a second fly fished with another rod—this would definitely confound the argument that salmon fishing is cruel! But this behaviour, whatever the reason for it may be, is most valuable to the fisherman, for it gives him time to get on terms with the fish.

Should you tighten now? Yes, you can do this safely, because you are now out of the water and able to follow the fish wherever he sees fit to go, and you are also below him, which makes it reasonably sure that when you do tighten the fish will run upstream.

Your whole object now is *to make the fish exhaust himself* as soon as possible. The old idea of playing a salmon was to haul away the whole time, no matter whether the fish was upstream or downstream of the fisherman. Our ancestors called it "fighting the fish", and they were quite pleased if they took a minute to the pound in bringing the fish to gaff; nowadays we think little of rendering a fish dead-beat in half that time, on very much finer tackle. Nothing could be better calculated to prolong a fight than this indiscriminate hauling. If the fish is upstream of the fisherman, a heavy strain will simply bring him down, and, if he is below, any strain at all simply serves to support him against the current. It is a hopeless mistake to imagine that if you are pulling against the salmon, the salmon is necessarily exerting himself to pull against you; a salmon cannot swim backwards like an eel.

It is not pain or loss of blood that brings the salmon within the reach of the gaff. It is exhaustion—nothing else. And the quickest way to exhaust the salmon is to annoy him into doing it himself. Put yourself in the position of the ju-jitsu expert who uses the *other* man's strength to beat him with. The purpose of strain is not to keep the hook in, nor to skull-drag the fish ashore (a salmon is much too strong for that), but to irritate him into running.

Now the salmon's natural reaction to having his head pulled in one direction is to fight away in the opposite direction. And the direction in which he will soonest get winded is upstream, where he will have to fight against the fast water. To make the salmon run upstream is the whole object of keeping below him.

Get him moving by pulling his head firmly sideways. All you want to do is to upset his balance—to turn him slightly, so that the current bears more on one side of him than on the other and sweeps him out of position.

He won't move? Pull at him again in steady jerks. Stand by to dip your rod point if he jumps. Good! Had you not "saluted" him then, that long slattering leap might have resulted in a broken cast. The shake of a salmon's head or a blow of his tail *while he is in the air* is too sudden a thing to be absorbed by the spring of the rod; safety lies only in letting the line go instantly as slack as possible. Get your rod up again as soon as he has hit the water. The butt of the rod should never be at less than seventy degrees to the line while a fish is being played. With the butt in that position it is impossible for the line to be pulled hard enough to break the cast.

Away goes the fish now like an express train right up through the waist of the pool. Let him have all the line he wants, but follow him up as quick as you can, so that he does not run it all out. He has stopped somewhere in the tail of the run. Give him another pull and get him on the move. Up he goes again.

Wait a moment! That snag, that you caught your fly in as you were fishing down, is not far from where the fish is now. Get above him quickly and give him a pull from upstream. That may send him down.

It hasn't! He's off again, and he's still going up. Hold him as hard as you can, now, in towards your own bank; you are using heavy tackle and this is one of the occasions where a strong strain is useful. Yes, I know you can put on more strain by lowering the rod point, but it is not safe. Keep the point *up*. You have turned him. The heavy water and the strong sideways pull combined were too much for him and he is shooting back downstream.

After him! Let him have all the line he wants, and he may turn of his own accord. Down he goes, through the dub and the waist, and on through the tail, past the place where you hooked him, leaving us scrambling along far behind. This is getting serious—not much line left, and there is a rapid below this pool; if he gets into that we shall never see him again. It is no use trying to stop him by brute force, as we did in the run. He's got the current with him now, not against him. We must try what cunning will do.

Put on a firm strain by pressing a finger on the coiled line in the reel. Harden it now, keeping the rod well back. Then suddenly drop the rod point, and tear line off the reel as fast as you can and let it go.

He has stopped, almost on the lip of the rapid. The sudden slackening of the strain has given him the impression that he is free. The slack line floats past him, and when there is a big loop of it below him, you give the rod a jerk, and the downstream pull brings him slowly up. He starts boring and jigging in the deep water, and now, while we are getting our breath, I want to revert to what might have happened had the line got foul of that snag near the head of the pool.

If the fish had got the line round the snag, and no

amount of pulling would have induced him to come back, there would still have been a chance of catching him and saving your line. If it had been possible to cross the river, a pull from the opposite side might have freed the line. Or if there had been another fisherman on the opposite bank, he would probably have been kind enough to cast his fly over your line and free it for you. If neither of these chances had been available, the last resort would have been to cut the backing at the splice or as near it as the length of line in the water would allow, and let the tapered line go, tie a stone, or a lead if you happen to have one, on the end of the backing and a couple of big flies just above it, and "fish" for the tapered line somewhere between the snag and the salmon. This may sound rather far-fetched, but in point of fact it would have been well-nigh certain to succeed, provided the fish stayed still, for your im-provised grapnel would have covered the whole stream and would have crossed the jettisoned line and caught it if it were still there. And if you could have avoided jerking the fish while getting the line in, the chances are that he would have kept still and you would have been able to connect up and resume the battle.

You want to draw my attention to the fact that the salmon has now apparently riveted himself to the bot-tom of the pool? You can't shift him? Have you tried hand-lining? If there were a boat in this pool, I would suggest rowing off and hand-lining him from directly over his head—that often brings up a sulking fish. As it is, we will throw stones at him. Strictly speaking, it is illegal to throw stones at a salmon. The Salmon and Freshwater Fisheries Act of 1923 says that no one must "use a light or throw any missile into the water or use any fish roe for the purpose of taking Salmon or Trout", and that anyone who does so shall be liable to a fine not exceeding £50, and, in the case of a "continuing offence", to still more drastic penalties. Whether that means £50 for the first stone and £50 for each succeeding stone, is not made clear, but if so it will cost us a lot of money to wake this fish up. However, I don't think even a High Court judge, if he came to hear of our performances, would do anything but commend us for our perseverance. In any case, there seems no prospect of our "taking this salmon by throwing stones at him", because for all the attention he pays he might be a stone himself.

Apart from waiting till the salmon sees fit to move, there is a further stratagem for waking him up, which generally works, but which is only to be recommended as a last resort, owing to the danger of subsequently breaking the cast. This is to make a traveller and let it slide down the line on to the fish's nose. Use a small stone and attach it to the line with a piece of twine and a paper-clip, just as you did the piece of wood for freeing the fly from the snag.

That woke him up. Away he goes, this time all over the pool, trying to get away from the stone that unaccountably pursues him and now and then flaps maddeningly against his head. He makes one more long run out into the fast water, you turn him from the snag as you did before, and find that you can draw him towards your own bank.

Work him down to that patch of shingle, reeling up as you go. Very often the vibration of the check of the reel maddens the fish and starts it off again, and if you are bringing a salmon in to be gaffed by someone else it is safer not to use the reel for the last few yards, but to walk backwards and play the fish in. The steady pressure is much less apt to frighten it.

You can see the fish now, moving feebly, now and

A 25-POUNDER FROM BARDUFOSS

WALKING A FISH IN TO THE GAFF ON A LEVEL STRETCH OF THE WYE

[*Bernard Alfieri Photo*]

then turning half on his side—evidently completely winded. But he may still have a kick left in him, so go carefully. Do not reach for the gaff until only a little more than a rod's length of line is left between the top of the rod and the fish. Then you can spare a hand to slip the cork off the point of the gaff and take hold of the shaft.

As a general rule it is better to wield the gaff with the downstream hand, and use the upstream hand to hold the rod upstream and keep the fish hanging in the current abreast of you. This ensures that the fish is more or less square to the pull of the gaff and gives you a moment or two to make sure of your aim. Some fishermen aver that holding the fish with its head upstream in this way gives it a chance to recover and involves the risk of its dashing off again before the gaff is in. They do exactly the opposite, and bring the fish down past them. But in order to bring the fish squarely opposite, it must generally be pulled faster than the water, and if it is brought downstream to the gaff it is being both pulled downstream by the rod and swept downstream by the current, which means that the fisherman only has a moment in which to clip the gaff into it. To do this, one has to be very skilled in using a gaff, and I do not think that the objection to the former method is a very serious one.

When the fish is opposite to you, reach the gaff over him, drop the point of the rod, and at the same time jerk the point of the gaff into the fish just abaft the dorsal fin, and with a rather slower continuation of that movement lift him ashore. The object of dropping the rod as you draw the gaff home is to avoid risk of the cast being broken if the fish should splash suddenly and drop off the gaff. For the same reason be careful not to pull the fish's head out of water whilst working him in. A fish weighs nothing in the water; in the air it weighs a good deal, and its movements are faster into the bargain, having nothing to absorb them.

Whatever you do, do not gaff over the cast. The cast must not be between the gaff and the fish, for if it is and the stroke misses or the fish suddenly rushes away, the cast will probably catch in the gaff and break.

There is still some division of opinion as to whether the fish should be gaffed over the back or under the belly. I think there can be no doubt that the former is the better way, because there is far less risk of touching the fish before the gaff goes in. Never attempt to "bring the fish over the gaff", as I have seen suggested—not only is it far more difficult to bring the fish over the gaff than it is to reach the gaff over the fish; but there is every chance that in the course of the manœuvre the fish will touch the point of the gaff and dash away.

I prefer to gaff the fish slightly abaft the dorsal fin, so that the gaff shall, to a certain extent, prevent the fish flapping whilst it is being carried ashore. If it is gaffed in the middle or in the head, its tail is left free to flap about and it may jerk itself off the gaff.

As a means of landing salmon, a gaff is infinitely preferable to a net. Not only is a net, of the size necessary to hold a salmon, a hopelessly unwieldy thing to carry about; it is also impossible to hold with one hand against anything of a current. If you ever do have to use a net, try to hold it open against the current long enough to let the salmon drop into it, and then at once turn the ring flat so that the salmon cannot escape, and you can then safely let the current take charge of both net and fish while you use the long shaft simply as a means of towing them both ashore.

On many rivers, at certain times of the year, and especially in early spring, a gaff is prohibited, on account of the large number of kelts, or spawned fish, which are apt to be caught at such times and which have to be returned to the water. A tailer is then the best means of landing fish. This is simply a running noose of stiff wire, which can be attached to the wading staff in place of the gaff hook. To land a fish with it, simply slip it well over the fish's tail and draw tight.

It is often not a difficult matter to tail a salmon by hand. The palm of the hand should be turned towards the head of the fish, the thumb and forefinger towards the tail, so that the slightly splayed cartilage or "knuckle" which a salmon has at the base of its caudal fin rests firmly on your thumb and forefinger when you catch hold of the fish.

Where there is a patch of gently sloping shingle, an even simpler way of bringing a salmon ashore, after playing it to a standstill, is by beaching it. Make a groove with your heel in the shingle on the edge of the water, and walk the salmon up into it. The salmon will probably start kicking when it feels itself in shallow water, but as its head is pointing inland any kick which it gives simply helps it further forward up the beach.

It is better not to use a gaff when fishing early in the year, for it is often impossible to tell, while a fish is still in the water, whether it is a clean fish or a kelt. Once the fish is out of the water, you have a chance of seeing to which category it belongs. In general appearance a clean fish is silvery, plump, and shapely. Its head appears to be small, but this is due to the plumpness of its body. The fins are dark, and it has very little in the way of teeth. A kelt, on the other hand, is generally a lean-looking brute with an apparently large head and teeth like needles. There are often freshwater parasites in its gills. Its fins are ragged and worn from much lying on the bottom of the river, with very often a marked redness on the lower ray of the tail fin. And the vent is slack, not hard like that of a fresh-run fish.

Always treat a kelt as gently as possible. It was probably in a weak condition before you hooked it, after its long journey, its nine months' fast, and the effort of spawning; and being played and carelessly handled may well prove the last straw. Wet your hands before handling it, so as to remove as few scales as possible, and, whilst unhooking it, kneel down and clasp it between your knees so that it cannot thrash about and damage itself. If there is a patch of shallow water near by, this can even be done in the water and the fish will be all the better for not being brought ashore. When the hook is out, put the fish back into the river as carefully as possible, holding it, if it seems much exhausted, with its head upstream for a moment or two, when it will probably swim off.

If you decide that your fish is clean-run, kill it at once by a smart rap with the priest between the eyes. Jot down in a notebook its weight or measurements (length and girth), and as many details affecting its capture as possible. The date, the names of the river, the beat, and the pool, the height of the water, the place in the pool where the fish took hold, the weather and light, and the temperature of the air and water— these details are too numerous and too important to be trusted to memory. Put them down at once; they may make all the difference to your fishing next day or next year.

There is one more rite to be performed. I am not referring to the "guid auld Scottish custom", which has to do with the uncorking of the flask (if you have a gillie with you, that is a rite that should certainly not be forgotten). What I am thinking of is the necessity of destroying the beauty of the fish, its unblemished loveliness and so on, in order to make it fit to eat. If you would know, or have your friends know, how a salmon should taste, harden your heart and look your last on what is certainly one of the most beautiful sights in the world, and push your knife through the body just behind the gill-covers. Then lay the fish away in the shade to bleed and stiffen.

Bringing salmon home is often something of a problem. Chaytor recommends floating them down the river on the end of a string. This is all very well if the banks are clear or the water shallow enough to wade, and if you happen to want to go down the river, but for getting the fish home one must provide some way of carrying them. A carpenter's frail is as good as anything else. An even simpler way is to improvise a carrier with a piece of blind-cord rather longer than the fish. Knot one end round the tail and the other end round the jaw, after passing it through the gill-cover. Then, for a handle, cut a stout piece of stick nearly as long as the fish, make a deep notch in each end, and slip the stick lengthwise under the string, letting the string lie along the top of it and in the notches. The stick makes a comfortable handle to protect your fingers from the string, and its length prevents the fish from sagging and stiffening into too unsightly a curve.

CHAPTER IX

PACKING AND COOKING SALMON

Pray let me entreat you to use no other sauce than the water in which he was boiled. I assure you that this is the true Epicurean way of eating fresh salmon.

SIR HUMPHRY DAVY, *Salmonia*

A SALMON, like every other fish and the parts thereof, not excepting even the roe of the sturgeon, is best eaten within an hour of being taken out of the water. It has then a richness that it afterwards loses. Between the flakes of a fresh salmon is a kind of rich creamy curd, or jelly, which disappears after the fish has been a few hours out of the water. If the salmon cannot be eaten within, say, twelve hours of being caught, it should be left for two or three days in a really cool place—just as game, if it cannot be eaten immediately, should be hung until the bacteria have begun to break down the tissues and add a new flavour to the meat. But this second stage, to my mind, even in flesh or fowl, and certainly in fish, is in no wise comparable to the first. The first delicate flush, "all the devious brooklet's sweetness", as Richard Jefferies remarked in a rather different connection—although the sweetness of a salmon is redolent less of the "brooklet" than of the sea—is gone, and replaced by an altogether ranker and harsher tang.

It is well to bear this difference in mind when sending salmon away to friends. The sooner the fish is sent off, the better. If it is likely to be eaten within twelve hours, and the recipients are not fishermen, do not forget to mention the curd, or there may be a repetition of the disastrous experience that Chaytor records in his *Letters to a Salmon Fisher's Sons*: "At five o'clock one frosty March day I caught a perfect spring fish of 15 lb., and by packing him at once caught the six-thirty train to London, and he was delivered before breakfast with a message to have him cooked at once. My friend was a hunting man, but no fisher, and he told me a few days later that the fish arrived bad and had to be thrown away. I said it could not go bad within a week at least, and more especially in frosty weather. But he said that his cook, who was a Frenchman, had cooked it at once and sent for him to look at it, and that on opening the fish it was full of a nasty cloudy mould—the curd that I had taken such pains to get for him. He does not know to this day that he threw away a fish such as money could not buy in London. I only said that I was extremely sorry, but that if bad, some one must have stolen his fish in the train and given him a kelt."

A salmon is best sent whole, as cutting it up involves a certain amount of leakage and evaporation of the natural juices. For the same reason it should neither be scaled nor cleaned. The blood is all that should be removed, and this is done as soon as the fish is caught by a knife-thrust through the heart. For sending a whole salmon by train the most convenient packing is one of the specially made basses, rather like carpenters' frails, that are stocked by most makers of fishing tackle. It is well worth laying in a few of these before going to the fishing, as it is most difficult to improvise a good packing on the spur of the moment. The household can seldom provide a cardboard or wooden box of the right shape, and cardboard, in any case, is generally too light, and wood unnecessarily heavy. At a pinch, a box can be knocked up out of an old ply-wood tea chest, or a mat can be woven of rushes and string and wrapped and tied round the fish; but both these expedients take time and may mean the missing of a train, and meanwhile the fish is losing condition.

Before putting the fish in the frail, pad it well with bunches of nettles tied firmly all round it, so that the scales shall not be knocked off during the journey. It is said that nettles do not sting if you hold them tightly enough, but for dealing with nettles *en masse* I find a pair of thick gloves better than faith.

In taking a piece out of a salmon to send away, a section should be cut with a sharp knife square out of the fish, like a slice from a loaf of bread. The part of the entrails severed should be left in the piece and kept in the abdominal cavity by means of a wad of nettles stuffed in at either end. Then a thick layer of nettles is laid on a square of greaseproof paper and the piece of salmon laid on top and wrapped up tightly, the parcel being finished off with thick brown paper, a cardboard box, or a bass, according to size. It is worth remembering, by the way, that the parcel should be marked "Salmon"; failure to do so renders one liable under the Salmon and Freshwater Fisheries Act, 1923, to a penalty of £50!

Fish sent by passenger train between two points within the British Isles are rarely more than twenty-four hours in transit. If salmon are sent in hot weather on a journey that takes longer than this, it is practically impossible to ensure their arriving in good condition. If they are packed in ice, it will have melted long before they arrive, and there is always the danger that refrigerating chambers in trains and steamers may be too cold.

The flesh of salmon, when once it has been frozen,

THE FAMOUS DIRT-POT POOL ON THE TWEED AT CARDRONA

As simple to work with a greased line as it is with anything else. The fish lie towards the bank on which the photographer is standing. The pool is best fished from the other bank.

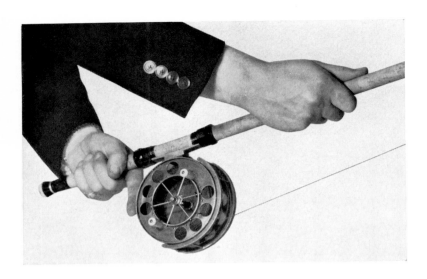

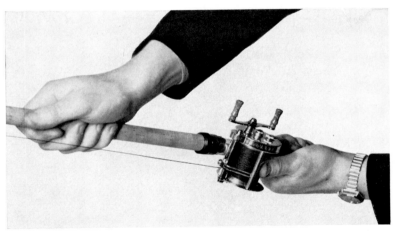

CONVENIENT POSITIONS WHEN CASTING WITH THE AERIAL (ABOVE)
AND THE PFLUEGER (BELOW)

Many fishermen like to place these reels higher up the butt, above the upper hand, to brake with that hand, and to tuck the end of the butt under one arm when reeling in. It is a matter of taste.

is as tasteless as wet cotton-wool. To preserve it in good order it must be kept at a temperature of between 34 degrees and 40 degrees Fahrenheit. At 34 degrees it will keep about three weeks, at 40 degrees about three days. For preserving a salmon for a long period snow is a safer medium to pack it in than ice, as there is less danger of freezing the fish; but it is safer in either case not to let the snow or ice actually touch the fish.

Salmon are at their best as food the moment they enter the river. They are then plump after months or possibly years of feeding in the sea and their flesh is pink and full of fat and almost savoury to the taste. They deteriorate steadily while they are in the river, their fat and richness going to form the eggs or milt, as the case may be, till a gravid salmon becomes as rank as a November stag. The time of year, and the distance from the sea of the place where the fish is caught, are good indications, apart from its general appearance, whether a salmon will be good eating or not.

In cooking salmon, the cardinal principle is to prevent the juices escaping. This can best be done by applying at once, before the cooking proper commences, heat intense enough to coagulate the albumen in the outer layer of flesh and so to seal the juices in. If the salmon is really fresh, boiling is out and away the best method of cooking it. Put plenty of salt into the water so as to raise its boiling point, and, when it is boiling furiously, put the fish into it. The coldness of the fish will bring the water off the boil for the moment, and it should be allowed to boil again and remain boiling hard for about three or four minutes. Then empty most of the water away, put a very little vinegar into the remainder, cover the pot, reduce the heat, and leave the fish to simmer for from fifteen to twenty minutes, according to its size. Six minutes per inch of thickness is about the proper time. Serve the fish in its own "juice", that is to say, the remains of the water in which it was boiled and in which any goodness that has dissolved out of the fish will be retained.

Grilling comes only second to boiling as a means of cooking salmon. The fire should be a clear red glow, and the fish is best cooked in steaks, the exposed flesh being covered with white of egg which congeals as soon as the cooking begins and seals the juices in.

An excellent way of cooking a small salmon in camp, when no cooking utensils are available, is to wrap it well in leaves or several thicknesses of damp paper and bake it in the embers of a fire. The cooking will be more thorough if the fire is made in a shallow trench and the fish laid on the embers, covered thickly with more leaves, and then enclosed completely with sods of turf. It will be two hours at least before the fish is cooked through, but it comes out smoking hot and so tender that it practically falls to pieces. Moreover the thick wrapping of leaves or paper keeps the juices in. A salmon is never more delicious than when baked in this way.

Frying is not always a successful way of cooking salmon. The fish is not oily enough to fry really well, and the usual mediums—oils, butter, and the like—spoil the delicate flavour of the fish. The skirts—the flesh enclosing the ribs—fry best, as these contain more fat than any other part of the body.

The two best methods of preserving salmon for food for a long period are bottling and smoking. Tinning is beyond the capacity of an amateur, as machinery is needed to make the tins airtight. Bottling, of course, can only be indulged in where bottles, fitted with proper airtight lids, are available. It is scarcely a suitable method for a camping expedition, owing to the weight of the bottles and their liability to break. But where natural baits have been taken in the usual square bottles with airtight lids, good use can be made of the empty bottles for storing a small amount of salmon. The salmon should be cut into pieces and placed in the bottles with only a small amount of water. During the actual boiling the bottles themselves should be stood in boiling water, otherwise they will be liable to break. When the cooking is finished, the bottles should be corked up while steam is still coming out of them and at once put aside to cool. The liquor inside the bottles solidifies into a jelly, and salmon cooked in this way is excellent eating and will keep for months.

Smoking salmon is a rather more complicated business, as some kind of smoke chamber must be manufactured. A packing-case or other large box will do, and it must be fitted with some arrangement at both top and bottom for regulating the draught inside. Juniper chips are the best fuel for making the smoke. Failing them, oak or ash chips will do, or even peat. Softwood chips are said to give the fish an unpleasant taste, because they are so resinous. The salmon should be cut into strips, and the strips threaded on strings hooked across inside the top of the box. The fire can be made in a trench in the ground under the box or on an old pan with holes in it, and the draught must be so arranged that the fire smoulders and does not flame. Smoking takes several hours, and the duration of the process depends to a large extent on the size of the strips of fish and the steadiness of the fire.

CHAPTER X

GREASED LINE—IDEAS AND OUTFIT

> But there is no accounting for the way a salmon will some-
> times take a fly.
> A short time ago, when fishing the Usk, a friend of mine put
> down his rod on the bank to go and talk to his wife. The fly
> was left in the water, and when he returned he found to his
> surprise a fish was on, and after an exciting struggle he landed
> him; he had been fishing that pool for hours before this hap-
> pened.
>
> MAJOR J. P. TRAHERNE, writing on "Salmon
Fishing" for the Badminton Library in 1885

SALMON fishermen owe a great debt to A. H. E. Wood,
of Glassel, for over twenty years the tenant of the
Cairnton water on the Aberdeenshire Dee and the
inventor of the way of fishing with a greased line and
a small fly drifted down just under the surface. While
fishing in Ireland in July, 1903, Wood discovered that,
in certain conditions, a salmon will rise to a small fly
drifting naturally downstream at the end of a slack line,
and furthermore that it will hold or chew a small light
fly long enough to get hooked simply by the pull of the
current on the bellying line.

These discoveries were made during a period of very
hot, bright weather when the river was at its lowest,
but Wood later found that at Cairnton the salmon
would nearly always rise when the temperature of the
air was above that of the water, no matter how cold
the weather might appear to be, and also that the slack
line would hook them more surely than a taut one,
even when the fly was fished deep. In developing his

114

methods he made further discoveries. He soon became convinced that part of the reason why salmon take a drifting fly is that they get a broadside view of it, instead of an end-on view, as happens with the orthodox sunk-fly technique.

To present the fly broadside means casting across and slightly upstream. But a salmon fly, just like a trout fly, cannot be made to drift down throughout the cast broadside-on *and* in a natural manner, if the line sinks. The current makes a belly in the line and you get drag at once. Wood found that the best way of controlling the fly sufficiently to keep it moving broadside to the fish and at the same time quite slowly throughout the cast was to use a greased, floating line, which he could "mend", or roll back upstream, as soon as a belly appeared in it, by a sideways movement of the rod.

Fishing in this way, he caught a large number of salmon during the years he was at Cairnton. In low water he caught many more fish than other rods, who used sunk fly; in high water, the same number, or sometimes not quite so many. In giving credit to the method itself, it must be remembered that it demands a good fisherman and a good deal of practice. It has been said that a sunk fly fished badly will catch more salmon than a greased line fished badly, even on a good greased-line day. Moreover, practically all of Wood's greased-line work was done on one river only—the Dee. The method is not infallible, by any means. It is suited only to certain conditions and perhaps only to certain rivers. But it will catch salmon in conditions where a sunk fly would be useless; it has shown us a number of facts about the behaviour of salmon that our ancestors would have smiled at, if put to them seriously; and, because a great part of its technique of fly-control can be used in fishing a sunk fly, it has added enormously to the interest and possibilities of that branch of salmon fishing and cheered the poor fisherman along what was formerly a rather back-breaking and soul-destroying way.

The greased-line method has two main objects: first, to keep the fly near the surface; secondly, to present it to the fish broadside-on and moving no faster than the current. One should remember that it is chiefly useful in hot bright weather and low water, though Wood found on the Dee that he could catch fish in this way even in high spring water and cold weather, provided always that one condition was satisfied—the temperature of the air had to be higher than the temperature of the water.

Now, as to the first of the *raisons d'être* of a greased line—keeping the fly near the surface—it is a well-known fact that salmon prefer a fly fished near the surface in hot bright weather. But there is some doubt as to whether this was what Wood had chiefly in mind when he determined that his line should float. I think his first concern was to ensure very accurate control of the fly, and this of course is best done by means of a floating line. The question whether salmon prefer a surface fly because they are gut shy, or rather line shy, did not weigh with him as much as ensuring that the fly should always come into the salmon's view swimming broadside-on and at a speed no faster than that of the current. In his opinion that was the vital thing. That the greased line did in fact keep the fly near the surface he seems to have considered rather as being incidental to the prime requisite of control than as being an object in itself. Wood did not believe that salmon are gut shy, in the sense that trout are, and that this might well be the reason why they prefer a surface fly to a sunk one.

116

It may certainly be taken for granted that salmon coming from the sea, the majority of them having never seen gut before, even as parr, cannot connect it with anything dangerous to themselves. They will often rise at knots in the cast, and Wood mentions taking one on a fly attached, by way of experiment, to the end of the reel line without any intervening gut at all. (But this was with a floating line, not a sunk line, and a floating line is far less conspicuous to the fish.) He thought it was all a question of proportion—that if you use a small fly on thick gut the salmon's attention will be attracted by the gut and he will let the fly pass unnoticed.

Crosfield, on the other hand, held the strongest belief that salmon are gut shy, and based his fishing on this supposition. In hot weather he used to skim his fly across the river, casting across and drawing the fly back very fast, not quite cutting the surface, his object being to make the salmon dash at the fly and take it quickly, before they had time to see the gut.

I think one should always give the fish the benefit of the doubt and presume that they are gut shy—not necessarily for the reason that trout are, but very probably, as Wood suggested, for the reason that the gut distracts them and they either move to the gut and not to the fly, or else the repeated passing of the gut over their noses bores them and they fall sulky.

American and Canadian fishermen are quite definite about this. They fish as fine as they can, sometimes down to 4X (17/100 mm.). In fact, some of them declare that they get more fish on a cast 20 feet long than they do on one of only 14 feet: I am convinced that they are on the right track, and that this is the main reason why the surface fly beats the sunk fly in clear and low water. If a fly is fished deep in clear water under a bright sun, the fish sees not only the fly but also the gut and probably the line as well. By fishing with a floating line the fish sees only the fly and the cast. It may see something of the floating line—how much it sees we can only guess because our eyes are not accustomed to looking up through water as a salmon's are—but it is certain that a floating line has far less effect on a fish than a sunk one.

The gear for greased-line fishing must, like all fly-fishing gear, be perfectly balanced, and it should be as light as the colour and size of the water will allow. In all fly-fishing it is chiefly the colour and size of the water which govern the size of the fly, and the size of the fly will determine the size of the rod, line, and gut needed to cast it properly.

One should never try to fish a greased line with a fly larger than No. 1. Besides the fact that it is going to be used mostly in clear water, there are two main reasons for keeping the fly as small and light as possible—you want it to ride high in the water, and you want the fish to keep it in his mouth long enough to let him hook himself. It is not only impossible to strike—in the trout fisherman's sense of the word—with a greased line (the line being fished quite slack); it is the most cardinal mistake a greased - line fisherman can commit, to attempt to strike at all.

Let us look into this. The fly must be small, in the first place, so as to ride high in the water. Now a salmon's mouth is a fairly bony affair, and there is just one place in it where you can be sure of making a small hook stick—the angle of the jaw. If you were to strike immediately a salmon rose to this small fly, ten to one you would pull the fly out of his mouth. But by not striking, by doing absolutely nothing, as the great shadow lifts in the water and curves down with your fly—about as stiff a test for a fisherman's nerves as was ever devised—you allow the pressure of the water on the bellying line to wash the hook into the corner of the fish's mouth and give the sharp point sufficient hold to prevent the fish getting rid of it. If the stream is of any strength and if you have kept your hook point needle-sharp, the pressure of the current will send it in over the barb at once. In any event, it is in the best possible place, and when you do tighten, in it goes. So now we come to the second reason why the fly must be both small and light in the wire—you want the salmon to keep it in his mouth long enough for the pressure of the stream to take up the drifting line and do its deadly work. The bigger the hook, the sooner the salmon will feel its hardness and spit it out. But a salmon will hold on to a small hook apparently indefinitely. Let the hook therefore be light in the wire—flattened, or oval in section. It should, of course, have a metal eye, and it will swim more naturally and hook better if the eye is upturned.

A hook with a shank slightly longer than that on which the usual sunk flies are tied has been found more attractive in this kind of fishing, but the length from the neck—that is to say, the base of the eye—to the outside of the bend should not be more than three and a half times the gape. A longer shank than this exerts too much leverage after the fish is hooked and is apt to tear out the hold.

The dressing of these low-water flies can hardly be too skimpy. No part of it should come below the level of the point. In fact, Wood had two "flies", which he called Redshank and Blueshank, which were not flies at all, but simply bare hooks with their shanks enamelled red and blue respectively, and with these he caught salmon. This sounds almost like magic, and both the "flies" and their names are reminiscent of the legendary tackle used by some hero in a saga, like Väinämöinen in the Finnish tale, who

> fished and tried his fortune,
> While the rod of copper trembled,
> And the thread of silver whistled,
> And the golden line whirred loudly.

Although pattern does not matter, so long as the dressing is short and skimpy, size is just as important as it is when fishing the sunk fly. It should range from No. 1 down to Nos. 7 or 8. Hooks smaller than No. 8 are hardly worth while—they take such a small hold that they lose more fish than they catch. But for very low water a No. 8 hook can be tied with a dressing no more than half an inch long, and the salmon will appreciate the dressing and not object to the hook— that is, until it is well and truly fixed in the angle of his jaw.

I have started by describing the fish's end of the outfit, because that, after all, is the most important. Having decided the rather complicated question what fly the fish prefers and how he likes it served, we can now work out the other components of the outfit, the gut, line, rod, and reel, without much difficulty.

The cast should be tapered, and its size at the thin end will depend on the size of the fly that is being used and the clearness of the water. For the small sizes, 6 to 8, I do not hesitate to go down to 20/100 mm. (the old 2X drawn). This will stand about 5 lb. and a light 12-foot rod can be used with it quite safely, *provided the butt is kept at a reasonable angle to the line, i.e. 70 degrees or more, when strain is on.* It is not practicable to go below 2X. Even a No. 8 hook, if used with gut finer than 2X, will work, as that great American fisherman, E. R. Hewitt, has said, "like a stone on a string", and the small breaking strain involves a rod too light either to cast the fly properly or to have much effect on the fish after it has been hooked.

Have the cast at least the length of the rod. I will go further, at the risk of incurring a smile, and say that 20 feet is not too much. When trout fishing I have always thought that a cast which is longer than the rod is nothing but a curse, but this is because the upper rings of a trout rod have to be made, on account of the lightness of the rod, too small to allow the knot between cast and line to pass through them freely. In a rod of 12 feet or so, however, fitted, as a rod for greased-line fishing should be, with large open rings, this objection disappears.

Now, as to rods and lines. On the whole, a single-handed rod is more convenient than a double-handed rod for fishing the greased line. It leaves the left hand freer for the frequent givings and takings of line that are necessary whilst fishing the cast. Also, the control of the rod with the right hand only is more sensitive than control with both hands.

The length of the rod will be regulated by the distance the fly will have to be cast. If two rods are of equal balance, action, and weight, the longer rod will, subject to obvious limitations, cast farther than the shorter one. The distance the fly will have to be cast will depend on the size of the river. In general, one should be prepared to cast 25 yards. Now a cast of this length *can* be done with a 10-foot rod. But a longer rod gives more clearance from the ground behind you and from the water in front. 12 feet is about the maximum length that can be worked comfortably with one hand, and if the balance is brought down well into the hand a 12-foot rod can be worked with very little more effort than one of 10 feet. It is not the weight or the length

so much as the balance that tells on the fisherman's
wrist. With reel and line attached, the rod should
balance at a point very little forward of the cork grip.
Weighted rubber buttons, made to screw into the end
of the butt, are often useful for bringing the balance
farther back without weakening the top of the rod.
It is a good plan to experiment with these if a rod that
you otherwise like seems a shade top-heavy. It means
so much to have a rod that you really enjoy using.

It is hardly necessary to say that the action should
be as lively and steely as possible. A rod that is in the
least degree sloppy or top-heavy is hopeless. Yet although the weight should, for the fisherman's sake, be
brought well back into the hand, the rod should play
right into the cork grip, and the top and middle joints
should at the same time retain their full share of power.
It all sounds an impossible paradox, yet so perfectly is
the making of these rods understood now that it is
only necessary to go to a really good maker to be
able to make your choice from a selection of first-class
weapons.

We now come to strength, which, in these days of
perfect rod-making, is practically synonymous with
weight. This must be adjusted to the weight of the line
which you want to use. The rod must be of such a
strength that it bends to the weight of the line just
sufficiently to be able to impart to it the full impulse
of the fisherman's wrist. Two sizes of line at least are
needed in greased-line fishing. To be mechanically perfect, of course, one would have a separate rod, line, and
cast, of varying weight, for every size of fly; and I
seriously suggest that it is only the shortness of one's
purse and the inconvenience of carrying all this gear
about that should prevent one's doing so. Wood in fact
used three rods, Balfour-Kinnear advocates three, and

Hewitt regularly took four with him, ready set up, in his canoe on the Canadian rivers. A canoe, of course, makes things much easier!

I cannot emphasize too strongly, however, that it is no manner of use thinking that one's regular sunk-fly rod—14 feet, 16 feet, or whatever it may be—"will do" for greased-line fishing, or that at a pinch the trout rod will be good enough. It will not. Try casting neatly even a No. 4 fly with a trout rod and line. The fly works, as Hewitt says, like a stone on a string, and it is no use substituting a heavier line, because the trout rod simply has not got the strength to work it. Conversely, a 16-foot rod, which with its heavy line will throw a 6/o fly perfectly, can scarcely be made to bend at all if fitted with a fine line and a very small fly and will simply drop the line about in heaps like a long string waved with a bean pole.

If you are going to try greased-line fishing at all, therefore, have two sizes of line at least and two rods to throw them properly. The lines should be double-tapered, and as to weights it is now enough to say that the AFTM numbers for each separate outfit of rod and line should be about #7 for one and #8 for the other. The first will deal with flies from size 8 to size 4, the heavier with flies from size 5 to size 1, thus giving a certain amount of overlap for changes of fly beside the water when for any reason only one rod and line is available. Note that in speaking of lines for this way of fishing the word "greased" is fast becoming a technical misnomer. Only if you want to use a dressed silk or "sunk" plastic line do you need to grease it. Far better dispense with grease altogether (for it is the devil to remove if the line is once more required to sink), and buy a line that is constructed to float of itself, such as an "Air Cel", now obtainable almost anywhere.

The two rods should be about 11 feet and 12 feet long, to ensure comfortable clearance for casting long distances, and the actual weights will be found to be about 10 oz. and 12½ oz. respectively.

Splice the lines each to 100 yards of undressed plaited backing and wind them on to two reels which are large enough to hold them comfortably—say, 4 and 4¼ inches respectively. The sunk-fly reels will do, fitted with spare drums of floating line, provided they balance their respective rods and hold the line with at least half an inch to spare between the coils of the line and the bars of the frame. They should have simply the ordinary click check, but it is a good thing if this is adjustable, as in using gut as fine as 2X it must be set very lightly—more lightly, as a rule, than the fixed setting of a non-adjustable check, though the latter can be modified by filing down the tongue, or, better still, having a weaker spring fitted.

Do not have a multiplying reel. The reduced power does not give one enough purchase to recover line against the fish with the reel only, keeping the rod at a constant angle. One has to pump the fish in with the rod, keeping the reel braked, and can only reel up while lowering the rod point. This lowering of the rod point whilst playing a salmon on fine gut is very dangerous. A rod at 45 degrees will pull three times, and at 30 degrees six times, what it will at 90 degrees, and you will remember we saw that with a properly balanced outfit 70 degrees is the minimum safe angle for playing a fish.

It is worth adding a further note on flies for greased-line fishing. The extreme variety of colour and consistency in the dressings of flies on which salmon could be caught had led to the conclusion that the details of the dressing were of relatively little importance, provided the dressing was skimpy. The customary dressing in these islands is of feather, with a body of fur, herl, silk or tinsel; while the Americans often use coarse hair; and some flies are now dressed on plastic or lead tubes which slide down the gut on to a small triangle. There is also a wide variety of feathered objects known as "lures". Any of these wildly differing patterns would catch salmon in certain conditions; but until very recently no-one had much idea of what conditions in general required what kind of dressing.

As the numbers of scientifically-minded fishermen increased, their observations began to crystallise; and a beginning has now been made towards forming definite theories. Very briefly, the idea is that dazzle eliminates colour and enables a fly to be seen by the fish only in silhouette, so that the dressing can be black and should be sufficiently bulky to attract notice. Conversely, on a dull day, colour is seen clearly, and a change in colour may prove attractive. The whole matter is dealt with at some length in R. V. Righyni's book *Salmon Taking Times*, with a most interesting commentary by Terry Thomas. As both writers admit, the development of salmon fly dressings is still very experimental.

CHAPTER XI

FISHING THE GREASED LINE

Oh! gently let the good line flow,
And gently wile it home . . .
                    THOMAS TOD STODDART

FISHING the floating line depends even more than fishing the sunk line on that indefinable art of controlling the movements of the fly which Wood called "watermanship". It is an immense asset to the sunk - fly fisherman, freeing him from the old mechanical technique, giving him an interest in the currents and vagaries of the water he is fishing, and making his work a much more positive and enthralling business. But in fishing the greased line, watermanship is necessary, I should say, not in a higher but in a more delicate degree. The floating line makes it easier, but the water is clearer and lower and there is less room for mistake. When a shadow materialises beneath the drifting fly, hangs there an instant, then turns with a flash of silver and disappears, as if remembering that it had a prior engagement elsewhere, that is the time for the greased-line fisherman to reel up and wonder what he is doing wrong.

Exactly why salmon are attracted by a fly, fished in the greased-line way, is difficult to understand. Experience, not theory, tells us what we have to do—keep the fly near the surface, make it move at the speed of the water it is in, and prevent its dragging. Yet at the same time we are faced with the undoubted facts that

126

in slow water it pays to work the fly, that a fish can often be induced to snap at a fly pulled up past it, and that the essence of the low-water tactics, made famous by Chaytor and Crosfield, was to drag the fly across the surface of the stickle at quite a rapid rate.

Of course, greased-line tackle is very fine—probably finer than either Chaytor or Crosfield used—and it may be that the dragging of the fly at the surface, and Wood's own tactics of working it in still water, succeeded because the salmon has to dash at the fly before he has time to notice the gut. I am sure that unnecessary thickness of gut accounts for far more disappointments than we realise.

Apart from that, the reason behind the success of the greased line seems to be that it gives the fisherman scope for experiment. By enabling him to make the fly behave in a variety of ways, it enables him to suit the fish's mood. Granted that a salmon does not take anything unless it wants to eat it, it is often particular about how its food is served. Sometimes it will rush at a bunch of worms from yards away, or rise quietly and steadily to a hatch of March Browns, like any hungry trout; at other times a fly may be offered to it in six different ways and be taken only at the seventh. There is no saying what a salmon will do. Any generalisation can only be a very rough guide, and the fisherman must keep an open mind and as many shots in his locker as possible.

I seem to have digressed from the subject, but it is important—if only for the sake of one's sanity—to understand what is behind all these apparently completely contradictory methods. The greased line enables you to *control* the fly much more easily than you can with a line that sinks. Wood found, on his own water on the Dee, that it paid best to fish the fly without any drag at all; but that on the Ugie, which is a still water, it paid to drag it. The basic idea of greasing this line was to enable him to do either, as conditions seemed to demand.

Let us grease our line, too, then (unless we have one that floats anyway), and go down to the river. If we have to use grease, a heavy grease, like Cerolene, is the best sort to use. Deer fat is too waxy, and does not make a thick enough coating on a heavy line to keep it long afloat. 30 yards of line should be pulled off the reel, the end tied to something solid, and the grease plastered on to the stretched line good and thick with a rag. Do not let the grease get on to the cast. This may happen during the day, owing to the grease slipping down from the fly, or the gut touching the greasy line, but if it does and the cast begins to float, clean the cast off with a rag soaked in detergent; detergent is an infallible "sinker".

It is best to grease both lines and set up both rods before starting out. You may not be sure how high or coloured the water is, or rain in the hills may cause a sudden rise of water, or there may be some other reason why a big change in the size of the fly becomes necessary, and even though you cannot carry both rods with you while actually fishing, you can leave the second one with the gillie or beside the pool or fishing hut, where it can be got at without much delay.

You will generally know from the feel of the weather and the look of the water whether it is a good greased-line day, that is to say, whether the temperature of the air is higher than that of the water—the essential condition for greased-line fishing. It may be one of those smiling cloudless days in early spring, that so strangely presage the summer, when the earth stirs beneath its dazzling mantle of snow, the midges dance outside the porch, and the thermometer on the wall will show 80 degrees by midday. That is a perfect greased-line day, even though the black water is only a degree or two above freezing-point and there is still a brash of ice along the pool edges. Or, the wind may have changed into the west, bringing sudden mildness and damp after a spell of raw-edged haar. The deduction from these conditions is obvious.

Sometimes it is not so easy. The converse occurs most often later in the year, in the evening of a warm summer day. In the gloaming the air still feels warm, but even so it is losing the day's heat more quickly than the water, and soon its temperature is the lower of the two. The fish go down, and the reason is not apparent until the wise fisherman remembers his thermometer, compares the two temperatures, and commends his solution of the phenomenon with a self-satisfied smile. It is *very important* to have a thermometer always handy—often it is the only infallible guide. A difference of only 2 degrees may make the fish ready to come up, or put them down.

In the early spring the fish will be in the deeper, quieter water, and the fast runs can be missed out. But streamy, spreading water, from 3 to 7 feet deep is best for greased-line fishing. The reason is that salmon lie nearly always within a foot or so of the bottom, and are less likely to come up from the deeps than they are from a shorter distance. Also, according at any rate to the laws of human optics, they can see through a wider circle of the surface from deep water than they can from shallow, and so are more likely to be distracted by the floating line.

Let us suppose the pool to be of that perfect and orthodox kind; a surging stickle spreading into a broad area of jabbly, streamy water, from 4 to 6 feet deep, over enough boulders to provide comfortable lies for a large number of salmon. Begin at the point where the surges begin to moderate. Cast a short slack line across and slightly upstream into the edge of the current. The fly will be in faster water than the line, and would, if you left it alone, be dragged out at once into the slack, or eddy, near your own bank. You want to keep it in the edge of the current, moving down at the same speed, for as long as possible. To do this, you must help the line near you to keep pace with it. Mend downstream, therefore, and keep on mending downstream until the fly swims *gently* out of the current well below you. Cast again, further into the current, and mend as before until the cast is fished out.

One makes much less disturbance in the stream by casting radially. This simply means standing in one place, casting a short line to begin with and lengthening it gradually until one cannot cast any further, then moving down to another stance. Very often this is the only plan possible—for instance, when one has to stand on a croy or a whaleback, surrounded by deep water. With a greased line it is quite simple to work the fly, even at a much greater distance than one can cast, simply by paying out line by hand after the cast is made and mending this fresh line as required. There may be yards and yards of slack in the water—it doesn't matter; the more the better, so far as hooking the fish is concerned.

The problems encountered in fishing with a greased line and surface fly are exactly similar to those encountered in fishing with a sunk line and sunk fly, for the objects, though slightly different, are achieved by similar means. In fishing a surface fly you want the fly to move at the speed of the current; in fishing a sunk fly you want to sink it right down to the stones, but you find that the best way of doing so is to make it, too, move at the speed of the current. The difference is that the greased line offers a vastly wider range of tactics for achieving this. With a sunk line you can only mend once or at most twice before the line sinks; but with a floating line you can mend any number of times during the same cast, and the water, of course, does not take charge of a floating line to anything like the same extent that it does of a sunk line.

Thus it is possible with a floating line to keep the fly for a long time moving gently in slack water beyond a fast rush, by means of continuous mending upstream. All the greased-line stratagems which have come to be used in fishing the sunk fly—and which I have described in the chapter on that subject—can be used in greased-line fishing with far more ease and effect. But at the same time they demand a lighter touch. Casting with a mend in the air, casting with a slack near the fly or near the rod, keeping the rod point high and upstream while making the cast, so that the intermediate line can be led down, and stepping downstream and giving slack to assist this—all these dodges can be used as and when they are needed.

Dragging the fly during the mend is less excusable than in sunk-fly fishing, and can be minimised by reaching the rod hand forward as the mend is made and giving slack to compensate as you draw back again.

A downstream wind can be used in conjunction with the rolling cast to blow the fly off and so create the effect of a mend; but this only applies to the initial cast. After that the downstream wind is a nuisance, for you cannot mend upstream against it. It is best, if a downstream wind is blowing, to fish the slow still water and use the wind to mend *down*stream, and so move the fly quickly across places where it would otherwise be scarcely moving at all. An upstream wind is better, on the whole, for greased-line fishing.

A greased line should always be cast slack, and kept slack. We have seen that in fishing with a sunk line, in spite of the necessity of frequently casting slack and giving slack in order to hang a fly, it is advisable to keep in as close touch with the fly as possible, in order to tighten on a fish before it feels and spits out the heavy iron that the sunk fly is dressed on. But with the small light fly that one fishes with a greased line, any attempt to strike is disastrous. The small hook will hold securely only in the angle of the jaw, and a slack line is essential for the purpose of sweeping it there. The fish will usually keep it in his mouth until this happens, as the wire of the hook is so thin and light that he does not seem to feel it.

When the fish rises, shut your eyes, if you can; be stricken, if possible, with gaping astonishment at the grandest and most fatal sight that salmon fishing can offer—the slow head-and-tail rise of a salmon to a surface fly: grandest, because there, taking your fly, *your* fly, is a fish bigger than the trout of your wildest dreams; most fatal, because if you have ever been a trout fisherman, the urge to snatch the fly—*out* of his mouth—goes through you like an electric shock. It must be resisted. Get into the habit of *dropping* the rod, if you must do something. But *don't* tighten until, long after the fish has gone down, the slack of the line has been taken up by the current and starts dragging on the water.

Even then don't raise the rod point. Bring it smoothly round downstream into your own bank, keeping the point almost on the water. This keeps the curved line in the water and exerts the pull on the fly from downstream. If you were to tighten by raising the rod, the line would be lifted off the water and the pull exerted from where you are standing, that is to say, at right angles to the fish or even upstream of him, and so out of his mouth.

In fishing out the cast, watch the fly with special care as it comes in to your own bank. Raise the rod point, at the same time paying out line by hand to compensate for this and so avoid dragging the fly. A fish that takes on the dangle is in the worst possible position for being hooked, for it has its head pointing directly towards the fisherman, and, being downstream of him, is likely to remain pointing in that undesirable direction. A salmon very often does take in this position, having followed the fly round from midstream and having decided to take it only when it seems about to escape. Any direct pull on the line tends to pull the fly out of the fish's mouth. The small hook must be brought if possible back into the angle of the jaw, and this is the object of raising the rod. The moment any suspicion of a boil is seen, drop the rod point at once and let the fish have a slack line, so that it does not feel a jerk. Tear off plenty of line and let the current take it down past the fish. The manœuvre is simply an application of the cardinal principle—letting the current hook the fish by pulling the fly back into the angle of the jaw. Don't tighten until the current has got hold of the belly of the line. If a fish is seen to follow a fly round without taking, give it a moment or two, before casting again, to regain its original position.

Though, in fishing across a fair stream, drag should be avoided like the plague, there are many situations where it is an advantage to drag the fly. Half-way down a pool, for instance, where the force of the stream is spent and the whole body of water moves in a sort of gentle drift, the fly would give the salmon too much opportunity for inspection if it were left to travel at the speed of the water. By mending the fly *down*stream it can be made to skid, and if the current is too slow even for this downstream mend to have an appreciable effect, the fly can be worked in slow even pulls by stripping line in with the left hand. Quite still water can be worked in this way.

Note that although the normal position of a fly fished with a greased line is just below the surface, when the fly is being fished without drag it does not matter if it actually floats; but if it is going to be worked, it should be sunk first by giving it a sharp jerk. Salmon do not like a surface wake in absolutely flat water.

It often pays to pull the fly off if a fish boils repeatedly and will not take; also, where you can get above a lie or a fish, to cast down beyond and to one side of it and then pull the fly up past it. Both these manœuvres have been described in the chapter on fishing the sunk fly.

CHAPTER XII

"DAPPING"

The clearer the water and the more shy the fish, the more I find myself fishing on the surface and playing the fly quickly.

A. H. CHAYTOR, *Letters to a Salmon Fisher's Sons*

In hot summer weather, when the water is low and clear and the fish shy, fly-fishing for salmon becomes a totally different business from what it is in the spring. In spring the river runs full and dark and icy cold, the salmon are all in the deepest water, and a big fly has to be sunk right down to them and brought across their noses as slowly as possible. In summer it is just the reverse. As the weather grows warmer and the oxygen content of the water diminishes, the salmon move up into the shallower, more streamy places, till in drought conditions they lie often right in the throat of a pool.

In this clear water the big fly of spring would be as terrifying to the fish as a Loch Ness monster, and a line —even a fine one—looks like a cable. A small skimpily-dressed fly is the order of the day, and the line and cast must be as inconspicuous as possible.

It has been found, by trial and error, that the best way of fly-fishing for salmon in bright low conditions is to fish the fly near the surface; but I think that the real reason behind the success of this method is not that the fly itself is more attractive in that position, but rather that, by fishing the fly near the surface, the line and most of the cast can be kept either on or above the surface, and so are far less conspicuous than they would be if they were sunk beneath it.

Roughly speaking, there are four methods of fishing a surface fly for salmon: the out-and-out dry fly, in which line, cast, and fly are all made to float on the surface; the greased-line method, in which the line floats and the cast and fly sink a little below the surface; the skimming fly, in which the fly and part of the cast cut the surface, the remainder of the cast and the line itself being kept clear of the surface; and dapping proper, in which nothing touches the water except the fly. The first two of these methods are described in separate chapters. It is with the last two that we are concerned here. The skimming - fly method is not strictly dapping, but it so closely resembles it, and dapping proper is so rarely used, that they can conveniently be discussed together.

I have said that I believe the success of fishing a fly near the surface lies not so much in the fly being near the surface as in the line and cast being kept as much as possible out of the water. Similarly I do not believe that the virtue of making a fly skim fast across the surface lies entirely in the attractiveness of a fly worked in this way. Except in very slack water, a fly is just as attractive if it drifts naturally down the current. In fact, the chief object of the greased-line way of fishing— which is primarily a low-water method—is to make the fly move at the same speed as the water round it. A skimming fly is attractive, no doubt, just as a sunk fly that is "pulled off" will often fetch a hesitating fish, but I think that the success of skimming a fly lies chiefly in its masking the line and gut. It lies first in the incidental fact that in making the fly skim *the line is kept clear of the water*; for whatever a salmon may or may not be able to see, it seems quite certain that a line that is clear of the water or floating on the surface distracts it far less than a line that is sunk. And it lies secondly in the fact that the salmon has to dash at the fly as it moves quickly overhead, and so is less likely to notice line or gut than it would be if it had time for a leisurely inspection.

The skimming fly has long been used as a means of catching salmon in low clear water. Mr Ernest Crosfield was perhaps the greatest exponent of it in recent years, but it was practised before his time. Probably it originated about the Border country, on the analogy of the wet-fly way of fishing for trout which is so extensively used there. It is impossible to pin its invention to any one man, but Sir Herbert Maxwell in *Salmon and Sea Trout* gives an account of a doctor who used a very close approximation to it and appears to have been such an individual character in every way that perhaps, in his part of the world at any rate, he was the first man to use it. The instance is worth quoting:

"At Reedsmouth, the junction of the Reed and North Tyne, there lived, in the days I speak of, a certain Dr. Begg, who rented the fishing of a couple of casts on the main river. 'Begg' is a name derived from the Gaelic, signifying 'little', and certainly it was appropriate in this case, for the worthy doctor could not have measured more than five feet in his stocking soles. When I first met him, early in October, 1867, he had killed upwards of 150 salmon and grilse with the fly during that season. And such flies! All of them nearly the same pattern—fat, fuzzy bodies, generally of gray rabbit or monkey wool, enormously over-winged, on small single hooks—and nearly all of the same size, rather large, and tied on collars of undyed treble gut. He very seldom left his house before midday, when, if the water was in order, he would get into a pair of enormous wading trousers, button his long yellow 'Piccadilly weeper' whiskers into his coat, clap on a cowboy hat stuck all over with hairy salmon flies, take his spliced rod, of the Castle Connell type, off the rack and stroll down to the river. Wading in almost to the armpits, he would begin on a fine stream which ran at the foot of his garden, ever since known as the Doctor's stream, flinging his flies (he always used two of these monstrosities at once) across the current at right angles and bringing them around to within a few yards of where he was standing. No low point and deep fly with him! On the contrary, he gradually raised the point of his rod after delivering the cast, trailing the flies along the surface of the water, so that when he had finished the circuit his rod was quite erect. Any orthodox salmon fisher who had seen for the first time Dr. Begg angling, would have set him down as an incompetent bungler. Yet, as I have said, he was remarkably effective."

Apart from the difference that the modern low-water flies are much more skimpily dressed than Dr. Begg's, his method of fishing is practically identical with the low-water methods used today—even down to the second fly, which is advocated by Hewitt and also by Balfour-Kinnear for certain occasions, although normally only one fly is used.

The flies for this way of fishing can be the same as those for greased-line fishing and are described in detail in the chapters on that subject. Occasionally larger flies can be tried. Sometimes, if the fish will not move, a turn down the pool with a very large fly will wake them up and make them take notice; and sometimes a large fly will fetch a fish that has moved half-heartedly at a smaller one but cannot make up its mind to take. But, as a rule, small water means small flies.

Many fishermen swear by double hooks for this kind

of fishing. They say that a salmon that is to snatch quickly at the fast-moving fly is more likely to be hooked on a double hook than on a single. Others declare, however, that the double hook, although it may hook the fish well when it rises, is apt to work loose during the play because of the leverage which each hook exerts against the other. They are both right, and it is impossible to assess the advantages and disadvantages of each kind of hook exactly enough to say which is the better. The best thing is for the fisherman to make a trial of each and see which loses him fewest fish.

Casting is of far less importance in this low-water fishing than it is in sunk-line fishing proper. Long casting is not only unnecessary, it is a mistake. The object here is not to sink the line but to keep it as far as possible clear of the water, and so the shorter the line the better. Therefore it matters far less that line and rod should suit each other. It is more comfortable if they do, but not vitally important, as it is in fishing a heavy sunk fly when long casts have to be made. The line must be dressed and tapered, as one cannot get even a short line out against a head wind unless it is of this type; but it should be quite light—the lighter of the two lines recommended for greased-line fishing will do very well, or even a medium trout line.

What is chiefly needed in the rod is length, for keeping the line off the water. It should be about 14 feet, and light enough to handle the fine line with some comfort. The cast should be as long as the rod, and tapered to 22/100 mm. (IX).

In fishing, cast square across the current or even slightly upstream, then drag the fly back, and down, at a good fast rate. In a really strong rush the stream does this for you, but in ordinary streamy water it is necessary to give speed to the fly by taking in line by hand between the lowest ring and the reel. American fishermen call this "stripping in" line; Crosfield called it "pulling through", but it is one and the same process, and the object of it is to make the salmon dash quickly at the fly, so that it takes it without noticing the gut. Not a foot more line should be thrown than is necessary, for as much of it should be kept off the water as possible. On the other hand, it is a mistake to wade in too far. A great deal of the art of this kind of fishing consists in balancing nicely these two considerations.

A development of the skimming fly method, in which two flies are used instead of one, is suggested by Hewitt in *Secrets of the Salmon*. The hook of the tail fly is snapped off at the bend and the fly used simply as a drag or anchor for the dropper, which is the fly that does the hooking. The dropper is attached to the end of the cast in the ordinary way, and the tail fly attached to 6 feet of fine gut, the upper end of which is made fast to the cast above the dropper. The combination is worked just as a single fly would be, the difference in the result being that the fly which hooks the fish can by this means be made to dance and dap on the surface instead of being only skimmed across it. If the "dummy" tail fly fouls anything while a fish is being played, the fine gut by which it is attached breaks without damaging the main cast. It would be impracticable to fish with two ordinary flies, owing to the danger of the spare fly fouling a snag while a fish was being played, and the possibility of hooking two salmon simultaneously—an event which would probably result in the loss of both fish.

Regular dapping, or blow-line fishing, is practised for salmon in some of the Irish lakes and differs little from dapping for trout. A long rod is needed and a light line of undressed flax. As nothing touches the water except the fly, the cast can be simply a yard of nylon of medium strength. The fly is a large, buzzy affair, very like the dry flies used for salmon on the Canadian rivers. A wind is necessary to blow the fly out and to ruffle the water, and the fishing simply consists in letting the fly dap gently on the surface. Most of the skill in this, as in other lake fishing, lies in knowing where the salmon are to be found.

CHAPTER XIII

DRY FLY

But when the Sun displays his glorious Beams
And falling Rivers flow with Silver Streams,
You now a more delusive Art must try,
And tempt their hunger with the curious Fly.
                    JOHN GAY, *Rural Sports*

DRY-FLY fishing for salmon is practised much more extensively in America than it is in the British Isles, and I think that the reason is to be found in the relative summer temperatures of American and British rivers. A water temperature of 60 degrees or over is necessary before the dry fly can be fished with anything like regular success, and British rivers rarely attain that temperature. Our warmest month is July, and the average temperature of the *air* during that month is only 62.7 degrees, so that the average river temperature is, of course, considerably lower.

Successful, though rather sporadic, attempts have, however, been made to catch salmon on the dry fly in the British Isles. Chaytor mentions taking a 19-lb. spring fish with a large hackled May-fly on the Tyne in May 1896; but adds that he did better with small lake flies fished wet with a trout rod. The first regular series of attempts to catch salmon on a dry fly seems to have been made by Major R. J. Fraser, C.M.G., on the Test, in 1906. It was a natural outcome of circumstances, for not only is Hampshire the home of dry-fly fishing, but salmon in a chalk stream are regarded as little better than vermin, owing to the amount of food eaten by their offspring which should have gone to fatten the trout. Major Fraser used a fly resembling a big May-fly on ordinary trout tackle, and fished it exactly as for trout. He had considerable success, although he soon found it necessary to increase the length of rod and line. He found, too, that he missed fewer rises by using double hooks instead of singles.

The great success of the dry fly in America resulted in Mr G. M. La Branche, one of the best-known American fishermen, visiting Great Britain during the summer of 1925 and trying out his methods on some of the best English and Scottish salmon rivers. Mr La Branche used a double-handed 14-foot rod, fairly heavy but with most of the weight in the butt, a tapered line, fairly fine but very heavily dressed, a long tapered cast or "leader", and a big buzzy hackle fly, tied as a Palmer, with the filaments of the hackle standing stiffly out all round it. The line and cast were greased and the fly oiled. The fly was fished upstream and across, just as it would be for trout, except that Mr La Branche showed exceptional skill in casting with either a right-hand or left-hand curve in the leader, according to the side he was fishing from, so that the fly came over the fish before any part of the gut or line. The results were rather disappointing. Many salmon rose to the fly and took it, but very few were hooked. The general opinion was that the fly was too bulky and that the fish felt the stiff hackles and got rid of it before the line tightened. However, this was not proved, as a great many salmon have been caught in American and Canadian rivers on flies of exactly the same pattern. Lack of practice may have had something to do with it, as Mr La Branche himself suggested, for he had not touched a rod for four years before he came to England.

There is still a great deal to be learnt about the application of the existing dry-fly methods to English and
Scottish rivers, but I am convinced that it will be used
to an increasing extent on the rather rare occasions
when conditions are suitable. Even more than greased-
line fishing, with tiny flies, and thread-line spinning,
with minute natural baits, the dry fly is a method for
water so low and weather so hot that any other method
is hopeless. A really high water temperature appears
to be essential, and, as in all surface fishing, the temperature of the air should be higher than that of the
water.

Flies for this fishing are very much in the experimental stage. The two types of dressing most used in
America are the Palmer and the May-fly. Both types
are tied as a rule on sneck hooks in sizes from No. 4
to No. 10. The hooks have to be light in the wire, so
as not to sink the fly, and made with exceptionally fine
and sharp points, so as to penetrate easily under the
small pull which is all that the fine gut, which has to
be used in this fishing, will stand. The Palmer dressing
is simply a close winding of long hackles, generally
brown or ginger coloured, with a turn or two of tinsel
for the body and a stiff tail made of whisks from a
smaller hackle, the finished dressing being sometimes
as much as $2\frac{1}{4}$ inches in diameter. The May-fly dressing
is much the same as that of an ordinary May-fly, being
made, of course, proportionately larger. Detached
bodies are often used. The patterns vary considerably.
These flies are not meant to imitate any living creature,
and the lights and shades in the dressing are varied
simply to suit visibility on particular days, and also the
whim of the fish, which is unpredictable and can only
be discovered by experiment.

The last yard or more of the gut cast must be as fine

as the fisherman dare use. Salmon have been caught on gut ·005 of an inch thick—finer than 4X. But this, of course, has to be used with a light trout rod; ·009 of an inch which is ·225 mm. or about 2X, is the thinnest size of gut that can safely be fished with a light 12-foot rod. The breaking strain is between 5 lb. and 6 lb. One should begin with this size, and take to a trout rod and finer gut only if the fish will not rise. The cast should be 20 feet long at least, for salmon lie lower in the water than trout, and so have a wider range of vision; and it should be stained, to prevent glitter. The light 12-foot rod and line, which I have mentioned as being suitable for greased-line work, will do very well for fishing a dry fly.

It is just as important in dry-fly fishing for salmon as it is in dry-fly fishing for trout that one should see where the fish is before beginning to cast. A salmon rarely advertises its lie by rising, as a trout does. The usual lifting or head-and-tailing of a salmon more frequently denotes a travelling than a resting fish, and in any case gives no exact indication where the salmon will be after it has gone down. One should look over the pool first and spot exactly where the salmon are. One then knows where to cast and can work out how the cast can best be made without scaring the fish. It is generally safest to cast from below and at about 45 degrees, and to throw always with an upstream curl in the gut cast, so that the fly comes over the fish before the gut, and with a slack line, so as to prevent drag for as long as possible.

Make the fly land 2 or 3 yards above the fish, and throw it, if anything, rather on the near side, so as to minimise the chances of the fish seeing the gut. The fly should be fished over two or three times without drag, and then, if the fish does not move, resort can be had to various dodges to wake him up. The fly can be pulled off just as it passes him, or it can be jerked under the surface at that moment and fished submerged for the remainder of the cast in the greased-line manner. Or, one can try casting from a different angle. There are no fixed rules, except that one must use as much care as in trout fishing to keep out of sight.

Dry-fly fishing is to my mind the most fascinating of all ways of catching salmon. If a salmon is inclined in the first place to take any interest in the fly, it is much less easily "put down" than a trout. Very often the fish can be seen from the place one is casting from, and then the fishing becomes exciting to a degree. The passage of the fly above him may make him settle down on his fins in disgust, but if he is seen to move his fins faster or rise a little in the water, then it is worth hammering away at him with every trick and change of fly one can think of. It is a mistake to give him a rest, as one would if a sunk fly were being used. If he shows any interest, keep at him, and sooner or later he will probably rise.

There is still doubt as to whether it is a good thing to strike when a salmon comes to a dry fly. Most American writers appear to think it inevitable that a great many fish should be missed, and this seems to show that the salmon does feel the bulk of the thickly dressed fly, and spits it out very soon after taking it. On the other hand, it is not always possible to cast from below, and it may be that most of the Canadian fish that are missed take below the fisherman—a point that is not made clear in the American writings. In that case, if the line were tightened at once, the fly would probably be pulled forwards or sideways out of the fish's mouth. I think that there can be no harm in striking at once if one is below the fish when it takes. The fly can, from that position, only be pulled back into the angle of the jaw. If the fish is abreast of you or below you when it takes, then it would seem best to leave the line alone until the salmon has gone down, and then tighten—unless, of course, the fish *turned* after the fly and its head was pointing away from you when it took hold.

CHAPTER XIV

SPINNING GEAR

You see the ways the fisherman doth take
To catch the fish; what engines doth he make?
BUNYAN

IN spinning for salmon, just as in fly-fishing, the
strength of the outfit depends entirely on the size of
the bait which has to be cast with it. Heavy water
demands a large bait, low water a small one, for
exactly the same reasons that these two conditions demand respectively a large and a small fly. In spring the
bait must sink deeply, move slowly, and show up well;
in summer it can be fished in mid-water, should move
faster, and should be so small as not to be alarmingly
conspicuous in very clear water. So that in spinning,
just as in fishing with the sunk fly and greased line, one
needs at least two outfits, one for big baits and one for
the smaller baits.

The interrelation of spinning gear, however, differs
completely from that of fly gear. A fly has to be flung;
a spinning bait has to be *slung*. In fly-fishing the weight
of the fly controls the *weight* of the line needed to carry
it out, and the strength of the rod needed to spring the
line. In spinning, the weight of the bait controls the
size of the line needed to let it go freely, and the qualities of the reel needed to let the line run. The rod, in
spinning, is of relatively little importance. Its pull must,
of course, be kept well within the breaking strain of
the line and trace, and a certain stiffness of the tip and

148

lissomeness in the butt is most convenient for throwing a bait, but, apart from this, the action and strength of a spinning rod need have little to do with the weight of bait or the size of line. A 5-foot rod will throw a given bait just as well as an 11-foot rod. It is the reel that counts in spinning—the reel, and the line which it must suit.

Baits can be either natural or artificial. Both, if they represent anything, represent small crippled fish; but a bait, like a salmon fly, cannot be said to attract salmon for that reason alone. In the first place, the rapidly spinning bait, that has been found most successful in salmon fishing, bears very little resemblance to any living thing. A crippled fish may lose its stability in the water and show the white of its flanks as it swims, but it seldom moves as fast or flashes as brilliantly as a spinning bait. In the second place, the predatory or feeding instincts of the salmon are practically dormant while it is in fresh water. All we really have to guide us in the design of spinning baits, as in the design of flies, is experience. The experience of generations of fishermen has shown that certain sizes and kinds of bait will attract salmon in certain conditions, but the reasons behind these facts are still largely conjectural.

The list of natural baits generally used includes sprats, loaches, eel-tails, minnows, and baby prawns. The first three are heavy-water baits, the last two low-water baits, although small loach and small eel-tails can sometimes be used with advantage in low water as well. Sprats may be either silver—their natural colour—or dyed gold. It is quite easy to dye sprats. Any good golden dye can be used, the scales being first scraped off the fish. But most tackle-makers stock sprats and other natural baits ready dyed. The golden sprat is the bait most generally used for heavy spinning early in the year. It shows up excellently in heavy water. The loach is a dull-coloured little fish, and is often useful as a change. The eel-tail used for spinning is the tail of a small eel; it can be used either as a wobbling bait, mounted on a single hook, or as a spinner, mounted on a flight; in either case the backbone should be cut out with a pair of sharp scissors before the bait is mounted. Minnows and baby prawns are low-water baits, pure and simple. A minnow is usually spun on a flight, a prawn either on a flight or on a single hook.

The preserving medium for natural baits used almost always to be formalin, but many fishermen are of the opinion that the smell of formalin is a considerable drawback, and that a bait preserved in glycerine or in a solution of sugar and water is very much less liable to make salmon "come short". Formalin has, however, a wonderful power of toughening baits and of fixing their colours, and it is advisable to soak them in formalin for twenty-four hours after they are caught, then to wash them thoroughly in cold water and transfer them to an airtight glass jar filled with one of the other solutions. Minnows and prawns can be preserved for a week or two in salt, either in a bottle or wrapped up in a cloth upon which a thick layer of salt has been spread. Baits can, of course, be used fresh, but preserved baits are usually tougher, and so get less knocked about by the inevitable jerks of casting and by contact with the bottom of the river and with the mouths of salmon; mounting a bait is a lengthy business, and having to do it often is not only a nuisance but a serious waste of time. Enough baits for the day's fishing can be carried in salt in a baccy tin. This is easier than carrying them in a heavy bottle, and any that are not used can be returned to the bottles afterwards.

Of artificial baits the two types most often used are the Devon and the Phantom. The Devon is simply a metal tube, shaped roughly like a fish, and fitted with a pair of fins near the "head" to make it spin. It is finished in gold or silver, or painted in various colours. The trace ends in a triangle or a couple of triangles placed in tandem, and passes up through the tube, so that when a salmon is hooked the tube is free to fly up the trace and so be out of the way of the hooks. A Devon is a useful bait in fast water as it sinks quickly and shows up well, but it is too heavy to be fished slowly enough in quiet water.

The Phantom is a representation of a fish and is made of painted canvas. It too has a pair of fins at the head, but the "arming" consists of from two to four triangles, on gut links, which are attached to the metal eye at the head and do not pass through the body of the bait but lie outside it. The Phantom is, of course, lighter than the Devon and so is chiefly useful in quiet water. For fishing it in fast or deep water, lead must be added to the trace, although Phantoms are sometimes to be had with a leaded pin inside the body for sinking the bait. The trouble with Phantoms is that they do not last; the canvas body soon gets torn, especially in the early months when the kelts are coming down.

Just as the surface fly has lately come into its own as a means of catching salmon, so it seems likely that the surface spinner, or rather "wobbler", may be largely used in the future. Many years ago American big-game fishermen took to using a "tarporeno" for "teasing" tunny and sailfish up to the bait proper. The tarporeno is a cigar-shaped piece of wood, with a downward-sloping scoop cut out of the front of it, which sinks it when it is pulled through the water and makes it wobble very like a limping fish. It was at first used without hooks, but the principle of the scoop made it move so attractively that hooks were soon fitted, and the bait became adapted to all kinds of fishing under the generic term "plug bait". Its great advantage is that it floats whenever there is no pull on the line, and so can be worked into a greater variety of places and at a greater variety of speeds than an ordinary spinning bait.

It is difficult to pronounce on the question which of the two types of baits is the more useful, the artificial or natural. I should say that natural baits are the more often used, and I personally prefer them. Although "unnatural" would be a better description of their general appearance in the water, they do at least preserve some of their original smell, and although, as I have said before, we cannot rely on a salmon's feeding instinct to induce it to take a bait, I am sure that it has a sense of what we call smell, and that that does make a difference. The texture, too, of a natural bait *is* natural, and that may induce a salmon, which takes when the line is slack, to hold on just that little bit longer which enables the slack to be taken in and the hooks pulled home.

Artificial baits are already "armed" with some arrangement of hooks, but a natural bait has to be mounted on a separate "flight". And here the writer on salmon fishing has once more the rather rare relief of being able to lay down definite principles. The flight should consist of as small a number of hooks as is consistent with their getting immediate hold, and the hooks should be placed where they will have the best chance of "hitting" the salmon when it runs at the bait. Constantly one sees flights fairly bristling with hooks— three or four trebles on one flight. Now it may quite easily happen, with a flight like this, that seven or eight hook points hit the fish simultaneously. The greatest number of points that the strength of the tackle will allow to be pulled in over the barb is two, or, at most, three; so that, if more than three points hit the fish at once, none of them will be pulled in properly, and the salmon will probably get rid of them at the first plunge. The ideal number of points for holding purposes is one. But unfortunately all baits, except the very smallest, mask a single point too much to make it sure of hooking. Triangles are necessary, in heavy spinning at any rate, but there should never be more than two of them. They should be arranged nearer the tail of the bait than the head, so that if a salmon comes a little late or snaps at the bait from behind he may still be hooked. The hooks penetrate better if they are fairly fine in the wire.

The other important characteristics of a flight are that it should hold the bait firmly and make it spin well even when it is moving quite slowly through the water. The latter requirement is met by large fins, set at a fine pitch. Transparent celluloid fins show less in the water than metal ones, and, if soaked in hot water, they become pliable, and so can easily be bent to a coarser or a finer pitch.

The power of a flight to hold a bait firmly against the fins throughout the jerks of casting depends on its general arrangement. The most usual form of flight consists of a finned pin, which is pushed into the bait's mouth so that the fins stick out on either side of the bait's head, and one or more short links of gut or wire, attached at one end to a ring between the fins, and at the other to one or more trebles, one point of which is hooked into the bait's side. In another kind of flight, called the Crocodile, the fins are fixed to a pair of little hinged bars, which are fitted with teeth projecting inwards, and are clamped down, one on either side of the bait.

But the best and simplest form I know is the tackle used on the Tweed. In this, the pin and the hooks are separate. The pin is fitted with a pair of celluloid fins and has an eye at its upper end. A pair of eyed trebles

PRAWN MOUNTED ON A TWEED TACKLE

is attached in tandem to the trace, with an interval of about 2 inches, and the upper end of the trace passed upwards through the eye of the pin. In baiting, the pin is simply pushed into the mouth of the bait and one point of each triangle hooked into its side, the gut being held in close to the side of the bait by the usual

THE TWEED TACKLE

binding of thin copper wire. The pin thus being free to slide, any jerk on the trace comes direct on the bait and simply settles the pin further into its mouth.

As usually sold, the Tweed tackle has one disadvantage—no swivel is fitted on the trace immediately above the pin. Most other flights are fitted with a swivel of some kind at the head, and to my mind this is essential. Turns form in any length of gut, however short, that is not separated from the flight by a swivel.

This is the disadvantage of those spinners, in which the celluloid fins are not fitted to the flight but are attached separately to the trace about a yard above it, the idea being to make the bait look more natural. Swivels should be of brass, and well oiled, and if of the usual barrel kind there should be two of them, in case one jams. Hardy's provide a ball-bearing swivel which needs a minimum of looking after, and is a great advance on the old design.

In mounting a bait, copper wire, about the fineness of sewing thread, is the best material for making the final binding which serves to keep the gut or wire, on which the trebles are mounted, close to the sides of the bait. Elastic loops are sometimes used, and sometimes gut, but wire is kindlier stuff to handle.

To make a natural bait sink in strong water, lead is needed, and fishermen still argue fiercely as to whether this lead should be placed in the body of the bait or on the trace some feet above it. The former way, where the lead is moulded on the pin of the tackle, certainly appears to be the neater. The lead, being out of sight, forms no counter-attraction to the salmon, and does not interfere with casting, as some fishermen declare it does if it is attached to the trace. On the other hand, if the lead is all in the body the bait will not swim on an even keel. It will always have its nose "in the air", especially at the end of the cast when the angle of the line is steepening. In very low clear water, however, the absence of lead on the trace outweighs this disadvantage.

The alternative arrangement — to have the lead on the trace—certainly makes more disturbance in the water, and it does occasionally—but only very occasionally and when casting into a strong wind— result in the bait doubling back and fouling the trace. That it ensures the bait swimming always on an even

155

keel far outweighs, in my estimation, those two disadvantages.

The swivel at the head of the flight will absorb most
of the turns that the spinner makes, but it is always
advisable to have some arrangement at the head of the
trace to prevent any turns, that do get into the trace,
from passing up the reel line. An anti-kink lead makes
the most effective "insulator". Where the weight required to sink the bait is in the bait itself, the anti-kink
lead can be quite small. There are many patterns. A
common form is a bullet, usually moulded on a wire
which hooks into the upper eye of the swivel between
the trace and the reel line; the bullet hangs below the
trace and compels the swivel to absorb any turns that
reach it. Another kind is the Jardine lead, which is a
long thin torpedo-shaped lead, having a spiral score
in it and a small spiral twist of wire at either end, so
that it can be attached to the line simply by winding
the line round it. When wound into the line above the
upper swivel, and bent into a slight curve so that it
hangs under the line during fishing, it forms an excellent anti-kink lead. A streamlined lead of this kind
is better than a spherical lead, which advertises its
presence by making a continuous "tear" in the water.
Any lead is far less conspicuous if painted a dull green.
Shaped glass weights have been tried instead of leads,
but they have to be much larger than leads of corre-
sponding weight. It has not been shown that they really
answer better, though glass "leads" and celluloid con-
tainers filled with water are useful on an occasion
where weight is needed for casting, as, for instance, into
a stiff wind, and where at the same time it is not needed
for sinking the bait once it is in the water. Where the
main weight is not in the body of the bait, but on the
trace, it can be in the anti-kink lead itself.

For low-water fishing, where even a small anti-kink lead would show up too much, a small semicircular plate of transparent celluloid, pierced with a couple of holes and strung endwise on to the line above the upper swivel, will swim without spinning and so prevent kinks passing beyond it. In using a gut trace it is always better to attach lead to the line rather than to the gut, as the chafe at either end of the lead would soon wear the trace.

Traces for spinning—for some reason the connecting link between the bait and the reel line is always called a "trace" in spinning, not a "cast"—can be of wire or gut. Many fishermen use wire, and much can be said both for and against it. Fine twisted wire does not kink and is very inconspicuous. It should not consist of more than three or four strands, however; there is a kind of twisted wire made of innumerable hair-like filaments which is as slippery and intractable as quicksilver, and should be avoided at all costs. Fine piano wire is said to be inclined to kink in casting, but I have used it for years and never had it do so. It has a fine springiness, which I find prevents it doubling back on itself during the cast, provided not too long a trace is used. If it does kink, it becomes hopelessly weakened and must be discarded at once. Piano wire is even less conspicuous than twisted wire, and it is easy to handle, and ridiculously cheap. A spool containing 50 yards costs about half a crown. The spool should be kept soaked in oil, as a single drop of water may rust and ruin the whole 50 yards. And the wire in the trace used during the day's fishing should be either rubbed over afterwards with an oily rag or else thrown away, for this wire is very apt to rust and the slightest speck of rust makes it untrustworthy. The disadvantage of both kinds of wire is their excessive strength. Even in the finer sizes this is far greater than any reel line, which is fine enough for spinning, and so if anything is going to break it will be the reel line. As the reel line is a level line, of presumably even strength throughout, it is just as likely to break at the reel as at the trace, so that one loses not only a flight, trace, and leads, but perhaps the whole of the reel line as well.

A gut trace is essential in very low water, being less easily seen than even the finest wire. And, of course, gut—or, as one should properly say, nylon—when used with a fixed-spool reel, becomes the reel-line itself; and it is so cheap that people seldom bother to make the "trace" lighter than the main length on the reel.

When using a flax, silk, or plastic line (*e.g.* with a multiplying reel), four feet is long enough for a spinning trace. There are two reasons why it can be so very much shorter than a fly cast. In the first place, a spinning line is very much thinner than a fly line, and so is far less disturbing to the fish. In the second place, the bait must not hang much more than 4 feet below the tip of the rod at the beginning of the cast, and as the anti-kink lead is better fixed at the end of the reel line itself than on the trace and cannot be drawn through the rod rings, that limits the length of the trace to 4 feet. Even if the lead is attached to the trace itself, there is still a further reason against making the trace any longer, and that is the chafe that occurs in the top ring at the beginning of the cast. Many fishermen use a short length of heavier line or gut between the trace and the reel line to take this chafe.

The traces that you buy ready-made usually have too many swivels in them. Only two swivels are necessary, one at the head of the flight and one at the upper end of the trace immediately below the anti-kink lead, though the top swivel can be a double one with advantage. This upper swivel should be just large enough in the eye to take the wire of the anti-kink lead. Swivels should be oiled pretty frequently, to keep them free from rust and working smoothly. To attach piano wire to a swivel, simply pass the wire through the eye and twist the end back in close turns round the standing part. It is less apt to ride up on the shoulder of the eye if the eye is first pressed into a slightly oval shape with a pair of pliers. Twisted wire would slip if attached in this way. It should be attached to the eye by a sheet bend, and the end then lapped round the standing part. In attaching gut to a swivel, it is always safer to make a loop first in the end of the gut, and then to pass both parts of the loop through the eye and bring the swivel back through the loop. The Turle knot is safe for small swivels; but the Cairnton often interferes with the free turning of the swivel.

The reasons for suiting a spinning line to the weight and size of the bait are quite different from those which relate a fly line to the weight and size of the fly. The weight of a line, which is so important in fly-fishing, does not matter in spinning. The momentum, in spinning, is all in the bait, not in the line. What the line must do, in spinning, is simply to run out with the least possible friction and resistance to the wind. Spinning lines are, therefore, level, and the thinner the line, of course, the more easily it runs. To allow a light bait to travel a long distance, the line *must* be thin. For a heavy bait the line can be a little thicker, but the *only object* of having it so is to stand the heavier pull which is needed to draw in the larger hooks with which the big bait is fitted.

Nylon has almost entirely replaced silk as a material for the finer spinning lines. Nylon lines with breaking strains of from 6 lb. to 8 lb. are most suitable for fine spinning for salmon.

For lines for multiplying reels silk or braided nylon floss are the best materials. Silk spinning lines, if they are dressed at all, should be dressed thoroughly, but with a very thin dressing. An excess of oil in the dressing is a far worse cause of friction than the water which clings to an undressed line.

Next to the invention of the split-cane rod, probably the greatest improvement ever made in fishing tackle has been the evolution of the modern spinning reels. The reel is by far the most important part of the spinning outfit. If the line could be coiled simply, safely, and exactly, without a reel, the ideal, so far as casting is concerned, would be to have no reel at all. As it is, friction must be as nearly eliminated from the reel as possible, and a delicate system of braking introduced, both to control the bait and to keep the stresses on the very fine line within a safe limit.

Spinning reels are of either the revolving-drum type or the stationary-drum, alternatively called the "fixed-spool", type. In the former, the drum revolves when the cast is being made; in the latter, the drum is fixed sideways to the rod and the line flips off the edge of it like cotton off a bobbin.

The essential of a revolving-drum reel is lightness in the drum. Inertia, rather than friction, is the bane of the revolving-drum reel, However smoothly a drum may spin when once it has got started, the inertia must be overcome at the beginning of the cast, and tends, at the end of the cast, to prevent the drum slowing down, and so leads to the drum giving line faster than the bait is taking it—the dreadful phenomenon known as "overrunning". Of the older designs of revolving-drum reels, the Aerial has as light a drum as any— a beautifully made cagework of aluminium and fine brass rods, turning on a steel spindle. The Silex, too, is a famous and excellent reel, the braking especially being beautifully designed and constructed.

In the more recent revolving-drum designs, such as the Pflueger, Rolex, Ambassadeur, etc., the inertia is cut down by reducing the diameter of the drum and so diminishing the fly-wheel effect. This loss in diameter is compensated by an increase in width along the axis so that the drum still holds the full 150 yards or more of line. The necessary speed in winding is maintained by multiplying gear. But a drum of this kind gives rise to another problem—that of distributing the line evenly over its whole width as the line is wound in. This is done by a traveller, consisting of a pair of small metal bars attached to a steel block, which moves from side to side on an endlessly-threaded spindle, geared to the drum. The line is led between the bars, and is laid evenly on the drum as the traveller moves to and fro. One would think that this arrangement would cause considerable friction when the line was running out during the cast, but in point of fact there is surprisingly little. Of course, the line does not bear against the bars when it is running out. It bears against them only when it is coming in and being distributed from side to side of the drum. When line is going out, the traveller passively follows the distribution already made.

In winding a line on to a reel of the Pflueger type, be careful to reeve the end through the traveller before attaching it to the drum and starting to wind. Be careful, too, when taking the reel off the rod, or putting it away, to keep an end of line always in the traveller. If the end slips out and the drum turns, the traveller loses step with the distribution already made, and synchronising it again is the very devil—rather like trying to correct the strike of a clock.

The term "fixed drum" or "fixed spool", applied to

reels of the Illingworth type, is a misnomer. In the modern examples of these reels the drum is not fixed; it merely remains stationary during the cast. The idea is to eliminate the inertia and friction of a revolving drum. The forerunner of these reels was the Malloch, in which the drum could be pivoted through 90 degrees, so that it lay either square to the rod or in line with it. In the first part of the cast, the drum was turned square to the rod, and remained stationary while the line flew off over the rim. As soon as the bait hit the water, the drum was turned back into line with the rod, and the line wound back in the ordinary way. Unfortunately, pulling a line off a stationary drum puts turns into it. The only way to take these turns out is to put the line back on to the drum in exactly the same way that it came off. That is to say, the drum must be kept stationary, and the line wound back on it either by hand or by a "flyer"—an arm which rotates round the stationary drum and lays the line back on to it. This the Malloch did not do; the line was wound back in the ordinary way, so that the turns which were put into it during the throw were not taken out. The drum could be taken off and reversed, but this only partly corrected the trouble.

In a modern example of a stationary-drum reel, such as the Altex, the drum is arranged permanently at right angles to the rod, and a flyer is fitted to put the line back in the same way that it goes out. This flyer is geared directly to the reel handle. The drum is free to turn independently, but is controlled by an adjustable brake, the tension of which can be altered at any time by a turn of a capstan nut.

During the cast the drum of the reel remains stationary, lightly braked. The line is disengaged from the flyer and goes out over the forward rim of the drum.

When the bait hits the water, the line is "picked up" and hooked on to the flyer arm, either with a finger or by an automatic pick-up, the handle of the reel is turned, and the flyer spins round and relays the line on the drum.

Now suppose that while the line is being laid on to the drum by the flyer a salmon takes the bait with a rush. In spite of the fact that the handle of the reel is being held and the line is hooked over the flyer arm, the line is still able to run out. For the drum is free to turn, although lightly braked. One can go on turning the handle of the flyer without danger to the line, even though the fish is taking it fast, because, although the flyer is trying to take it in, the drum will give it up. When the strain exerted by the fish becomes less than that to which the brake of the drum has been set, the drum will stop and the line will come in. Thus, the combination of flyer and drum acts as a kind of slipping clutch, by which the line is always safeguarded from excessive strain.

Practically the only disadvantage of stationary drum reels is the limitation in the size of the drum which is necessary to ensure that the line slips off easily. 150 yards of line is needed, and if a line of this length is to be got on to the small drum it must be a very fine one. This makes the reel less suitable for heavy work than a revolving-drum reel. It is an advantage to use a 12-lb. or 15-lb. silk line in early spring, simply for the purpose of pulling in the larger hooks which must be used with the big bait needed at that time of the year; and a line of that size cannot be accommodated on a stationary-drum reel. The stationary-drum reel is essentially for fine work; the revolving-drum reel for heavy work.

The least important part of the spinning outfit is the

rod. A good rod, of course, is always a delight, but what I want to emphasise is that a spinning bait, unlike a fly, can be got out with almost any rod, given a proper reel and line. The best action for a spinning rod is stiffness in the top and lissomeness in the butt. The rings should be rather larger than those in a fly rod, so as to reduce friction as much as possible, but there should not be too few of them; if they are spaced too widely apart, the bights of line between them flap about and create friction.

Very short single-handed spinning rods, for use with the wide-drum reels of the Pfleuger type, are popular in America and are used to some extent in this country. They vary from 4 feet 6 inches to 7 feet long and are fascinating little things to handle, but, to my mind, no other advantage can be claimed for them. It is said that they enable a fisherman to cast from difficult places, but there are very few places in which, supposing a rod can be used at all, there is room for a rod of 4 feet 6 inches and not for one of 8 feet. The small extra amount of clearance needed for the cast can generally be got without difficulty.

It is said, too, that the small rod is less in the way than the long rod; but the only place where this is of any advantage is a boat. It is not even true of the rod in a train or a car, because the long tip is generally made in one piece to slip into a socket in the butt, and is considerably longer than the joints of a two-piece 8-foot rod, which has its ferrules in the middle. In any river where rocks or bushes have to be encountered the short rod is a perfect curse. It may be very well in a boat, but for keeping the line off the water and clear of rocks and bushes, and for generally exercising control over both the bait and the fish, the longer rod is incomparably more useful.

164

The best spinning rod I ever owned is an 11-foot two-piece spliced greenheart, made of the butt and middle joints of a big old Castle Connell fly rod. Greenheart is safer for a spinning rod than it is for a fly rod, as the spinning rod has less strain to withstand and can be made so much heavier in the tip. The smooth solid resilience of greenheart is pleasanter, too, for throwing a spinning bait than the quick steely spring of cane, which often causes a bounce at the end of the drive, where it has no heavy line to keep it steady. But I do not mean to set greenheart against fibreglass as material for a spinning rod. The action of fibreglass is slower than split cane and it makes a perfect rod for spinning.

Spinning rods have butts shorter or longer according to the style of spinning that the fisherman intends to adopt. Those with long butts are usually provided with variable reel fittings, so that the reel can be shifted up or down and used either over or under the rod, as fancy or the fisherman's comfort dictates.

CHAPTER XV

SPINNING IN HEAVY WATER

Do not spin too fast, or you run away from the fish, but spin just fast enough to make the bait spin well, which it should do easily.
FRANCIS FRANCIS, *A Book on Angling*

THE whys and the wherefors of the heavy spinning outfit I have tried to explain in the last chapter. It should consist of a double-handed rod, between 8 and 11 feet long, a revolving-drum reel, holding 150 yards of undressed silk or braided plastic line having a breaking strain of between 12 and 16 lb., a 4-foot trace of level nylon of size 30/100 mm. (10 lb. breaking strain), with a double swivel and an anti-kink lead at the upper end, and, at the lower end a flight, with a swivel at its head and fitted with not more than two triangles of about size 9. If a fixed-spool reel is used, the monofilament line should similarly be slightly stronger than the trace —say 12 lb. The best all-round bait to begin with, supposing that the river is fairly full, is a 4½-inch golden sprat.

A fisherman using a revolving-drum reel for the first time would be well advised, before going to the river, to spend a few hours in practising on a lawn or in a field. There is a knack in casting a bait, just as there is in casting a fly, and it takes some little time to learn. Substitute a ¾-oz. lead for the flight and trace, give yourself plenty of room, and place spectators at a safe distance. Mark with a stick or a hat the place you intend to aim at, and go 20 yards away from it.

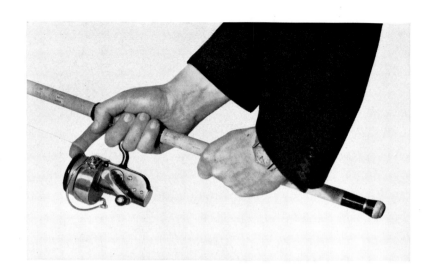

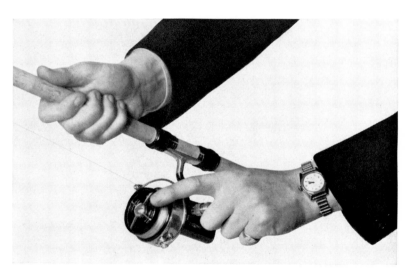

THE ALTEX-TYPE STATIONARY-DRUM OR FIXED-SPOOL REEL

[*Bernard Alfieri Photo*]

WHERE A BOAT IS A NECESSITY

Spinning in Lower Stobhall on the Tay at Stanley. (The fisherman is holding his rod-point too low.)

Now imagine that you are standing in the centre of a clock face and that the aiming-mark represents twelve o'clock. Stand facing two o'clock, reel up until the lead hangs from the rod point at the end of about 4 feet of line, and move the rod back to seven o'clock. Take the check off, and hold the edge of the reel drum by pressing a finger against it. Now rock the lead back slightly, and at once swing it *gently* round towards the aiming-mark, at the same time lifting your finger clear of the reel drum. When the rod is about three-quarters of the way round and the lead at the top of its trajectory, let your finger come back on to the edge of the reel drum and brake it with increasing pressure as the lead falls. The drum should stop turning just at the moment when the lead hits the ground, or the mark, as the case may be.

The chief difficulty at first is to time correctly the braking of the reel as the bait falls. If the pressure is too great or too suddenly applied, the bait will not travel its full distance, but will be checked in the air and will fall heavily. But this is a better fault than applying too little pressure or applying it too late. In that event the drum will still be spinning when the bait has ceased to draw out the line. In other words, the drum will "overrun" the line; and the line will pile up all round it in loose coils and form a tangle which scarcely bears looking at. However, an overrun is never so complicated as it appears; there are no knots in it; it is simply a collection of loops, and, if the line is humoured gently, they can soon be shaken loose. Take the drum out, if it can be done easily, and never jerk the line or pass the end.

It is only in a reel of the Aerial type that the braking is done by pressing a finger on the drum itself. In the Silex reels it is done by pressing a lever, and in the

Pflueger-type (multiplier) reels, which are best fixed above the rod, by thumb-pressure on the coiled line. But the timing is exactly the same in any revolving-drum reel. All such spinning reels have, in addition to the ratchet check, which is lifted during casting, a silent adjustable drag which is set according to the weight of the bait; for a light bait it is released altogether, but, in casting a heavy bait, a small drag imposed on the drum throughout the cast makes the finger or lever braking easier, and lessens the risk of an overrun.

During the first few practices the chances of an overrun are greatly decreased if you take care not to swing too hard. The swing can be hardened gradually—and the cast consequently lengthened—as you acquire confidence in your ability to slow the drum down at the right time. Do not forget to rock the bait back immediately before delivering the power stroke; this brings the body acted on (the bait) in line with the direction of the pull — the first essential in transmitting momentum to anything. As you pick up the trick of casting, you will find that in "getting hold" of the bait in this way at the beginning of the cast you bring the rod point very slightly downwards between about seven o'clock and five o'clock, and that the power stroke becomes a toss rather than a swing. In casting against the wind the reel must be slowed up sooner than in casting down wind, because, in the former case, the bait falls more steeply.

It saves much time and profanity beside the river if sufficient baits for the day are mounted on separate flights before one sets out. Mounting a bait is a delicate business and is better done in comfort indoors than with numbed fingers in a freezing wind when the fish are clamouring to be caught. The bait should be taken off again after fishing, and the flights dried and wiped over with an oily rag; if the baits are left mounted for more than a day the flights will begin to rust.

The tactics for fishing a pool in the spring with a spinning bait are very much the same as those for fishing it with a sunk fly. The main difference is that the spinning bait must always be kept moving faster than the water, so that it shall spin. A further difference is that the spinning bait, being heavier than the fly, sinks much more easily, and the spinning line, being thinner than the fly line, is not so influenced by the currents, so that mending and the other aids to casting, used in fishing with a sunk fly, can be dispensed with.

To make the bait come slowly past the fish, the downstream cast is the most useful. In deep water give the bait a moment or two to sink before beginning to wind up. It will be at the right depth as it comes across the stream if it is felt to knock occasionally on the bottom. The depth of the bait can be regulated to a great extent from the reel. But if it bumps repeatedly, in spite of being brought home rather faster, a smaller lead should be substituted for the one in use; and if it does not touch at all, in spite of being let go, a heavier lead should be used. Do *not* point the rod at the bait when fishing out the cast with a revolving-drum reel. If a fish takes with a bang when the rod is in this position, a smash will probably result, for there is no slipping clutch, as there is in a stationary-drum reel, to guard against sudden jerks. The only safeguard is to keep the rod at an angle to the line—preferably low and pointing towards your own bank.

The downstream cast in spinning, while it is a most useful way of bringing the bait quite slowly in front of the fish, shares, of course, the disadvantages of the same cast in fly-fishing. Unfortunately, owing to the necessity of making it spin, a bait cannot be allowed to drift, as a fly can, when cast more squarely across the stream. It must continually be drawn in, and this in a strong stream results in its coming round too fast. But the square cast should be used wherever the water is moving quietly enough to let the bait sink properly and come round reasonably slowly.

I do not think it pays to jerk the bait, except for an occasional sink-and-draw movement when the bait is at the dangle before the last few yards of line are reeled in. If no fish offers, or if a fish offers and will not take, change first to a smaller size of bait; then try a different kind.

It is not true to say that a salmon which takes a spinning bait generally hooks himself. Time and again, a salmon will pluck at a bait, in some mysterious fashion, without getting hooked, and those which do appear to hook themselves are rarely, in fact, hooked properly, until a good strain is put on the line. When the fish takes the bait, the hooks may penetrate sufficiently to prevent the fish's getting rid of them immediately, but it is only when the line is hauled tight that they go in over the barb. One has to remember, in spinning, that there is not one hook point, but perhaps three or four to pull home simultaneously, and that, when a large flight is being used, only a good solid pressure will do this.

The safest course is to strike good and hard whenever the slightest check of the line is seen or felt. An additional reason for doing so is that a spinning flight, with its fins and its armament of hooks, must feel much more suspicious to the salmon's tongue even than a heavy sunk fly. As the Shipwrecked Mariner was to the Whale in the Just So Story, it is probably "nice, but nubbly", and, like the Whale, the salmon will probably be very soon inclined to spit it out.

Giving a slack line, at any rate, is scarcely likely to help in hooking, as it frequently does in sunk-fly fishing and always does in greased-line fishing. The small pressure exerted on the fine spinning line by even a strong current is not sufficient to drive in the several points which may all be bearing on the salmon's mouth. A salmon which has taken a bait below a fisherman has been known to swim up with it past him until he was able to strike from below—the proper direction—but one cannot expect every fish that takes downstream of one to be as suicidal as this. In most cases the salmon would feel the "nubbliness" of the flight at once, and would try to spit it out.

CHAPTER XVI

SPINNING IN LOW WATER

The surest way
To take the fish, is give her leave to play,
And yield her line.
QUARLES, *Shepheard's Eclogues* [1644]

THE tiny baits which have to be used in low water—
weighing, some of them, when mounted, not more than
a quarter of an ounce—could never be cast with a
revolving-drum reel. A stationary-drum reel is needed,
and a 6-lb. to 8-lb. nylon line. It is not a bad plan to
take both these sizes to the river, the smaller of them
being wound on a spare drum which can be slipped on
at any time in place of the drum in use; if it is found
necessary to use the smallest baits, the slightly finer
line will add yards to the distance they can be cast.

The rod is a cut-down trout rod, or, if you feel so
inclined, a specially-made spinning rod (though this is
not strictly necessary), and the trace a 4-foot length of
level nylon rather weaker than the line, and fitted with
the tiniest of swivels and anti-kink leads. If the water
is exceptionally low and clear, the lead should be
replaced by an anti-kink plate of transparent celluloid.

The best bait is a 2-inch minnow. It can either be
mounted on a very small finned flight, or alternatively
arranged as a wobbler on an equally small Aerial
tackle, which consists of nothing but a lead which is
pushed into the bait's mouth, and two little triangles,
about size 9 or 10, which are fixed into its side in such

a way that the bait is given a curve. If a baby prawn is used, it should be mounted on a finned tackle with one or two small triangles; but a prawn—even a spinning prawn—should not be tried until everything else has failed, for salmon are often scared rather than attracted by it.

Casting with a stationary-drum reel needs little or no practice. There is no question of overruns, since the drum does not rotate at all in casting. The line is simply unhooked from the flyer, held against the rod with a finger while the bait is rocked back, and released as the power-stroke is made. There is no need to brake it while the bait falls, for when the bait stops pulling it out there is nothing else to make it come off the reel. When the bait hits the water, the line is picked up automatically, and laid back on the drum by the flyer as the handle is turned. Until a fish is hooked, the adjustable brake on the drum, or the slipping clutch, as the case may be, should be set at "striking tension", that is to say, a tension that is about half the breaking strain of the trace. In most reels this can be done exactly, as the tension in pounds is marked on the adjustable screw. The purpose of "striking tension" is to enable the hook to be pulled home when a fish takes, and, at the same time, to protect the fine gear against any excess strain in striking. The moment the hooks are in, the tension should be slacked off until it is just sufficient to prevent the drum overrunning when the fish is taking line. The purpose in reducing it below striking tension is to protect the line from the *sudden* jerks which often occur in playing the fish.

Spinning for salmon with this "thread-line" outfit, as it is called, in dead low water, is, for sheer fascination, comparable only to dry-fly fishing. A dull day is better than a bright day, but though air and water are full of

13   173

sunlight and a pool tail, 10 feet deep, is simply an amber shadow between your eye and the pebbles on the river-bed, you need feel none of that helplessness which fills even the trout fisherman at such a time. The tackle makes you master of the situation. The transparent line, thin almost as a hair, is difficult to see even in that crystal water, and the 2-inch minnow, with its arming of No. 15 trebles, comes towards you for a reason no more apparent than that which brings a pin to a magnet.

A thread line and summer weather is practically the only combination of conditions which permits the up-stream cast—the cast which gives the best chance of hooking the fish. The line is inconspicuous enough to be cast safely much nearer the fish than any silk line could be, and the relatively high speed at which the bait must be drawn to make it spin as it comes down the current does not matter in summer, when the fish can see it from farther away and are much more ready to go some distance for it, if they want it at all, than they are earlier in the year.

Do not cast directly upstream unless that is the only way a lie can be reached. Cast across as well as up at an angle of 45 degrees. Do not be afraid to let the bait come down and sweep round at a good speed, for, fine though the line is, the salmon should not be given an opportunity of inspecting it too closely. As a rule it should be fished rather in mid-water. There is no need to make it trip the bottom, unless it is used in low water very early in the year, and, on the other hand, if it is kept constantly at the surface the fish do not get such a good view of it.

There can be no doubt that there is something in the contention that thread-line fishing is easy. The bait can be cast accurately without difficulty, and the freedom

A 20-LB. COCK FISH IN FULL SPAWNING LIVERY

Note the great beak on the lower jaw.

A 22-LB. HEN FISH WHICH HAD SPAWNED BEFORE

Note the numerous spots on the gill-covers and the spots and speckles below the medial line.

SOME LITTLE ONES

a. Trout. *b.* Salmon parr. *c, d,* and *e.* Salmon smolts. In *d* and *e* some of the scales have been removed, showing the parr markings on the true skin under the scales.

as to the depth and speed of the bait and the angle of cast makes it possible to cover salmon which could never be reached by any other method. The justification for the method, if so delicate a way of fishing needs justification, is that, apart from the greased line and perhaps the dry fly, the thread-line method is the only one with which, in low water, salmon can be caught at all. Certainly one should never hesitate to use it. There is no cast-iron certainty about it, and one will never catch enough salmon on a thread line or any other line to interfere seriously with the stock of fish in the river.

Whether casting upstream or down, the cast should be kept as short as possible. The reason is that nylon stretches under strain sometimes as much as 10 per cent of its length, and so the longer the cast the more difficult it is to pull the hook into the fish. The length of the cast must be chiefly regulated by the strength of the swing, but if the bait is seen to be over-shooting the mark, a braking effect can be achieved by placing a finger near the rim of the drum and bearing lightly against the line as it flicks around.

When a fish is hooked the tension on the drum should at once be eased off, and thereafter the right (or left) hand should never leave the handle of the reel. When the fish is taking line, the handle should be held fast, while strain is exerted on the fish by braking the drum with the forefinger of the same hand. Whenever the strain on the line is less than that exerted by the adjustable brake on the drum, the line can be recovered by turning the handle. There is nothing to prevent the handle being turned at the same time that the fish is running, but, as the drum will not let the line come in until the strain falls below that of the adjustable brake, there is not much point in winding up until it does so. Note that, for this reason also, thread-line fishing is the one exception to the rule that the rod must never point at the fish.

Playing a salmon on 2X gut is not the miracle of skill which it used to be accounted. More skill is needed than in playing a salmon on any heavier gear, but so long as one remembers never to attempt to skull-drag the fish, but to let it exhaust *itself*, one should win every time.

Just as the technique of fly control was improved by the greased-line method, so the technique of playing a salmon was practically revolutionised by the thread line. One cannot "give a fish the butt" when one is using a 2X trace. The small strain that can be brought to bear on the fish is, however, quite adequate—for pulling it off its balance and keeping it on the move. The fish should not only be allowed, but encouraged, to run as far and as fast as possible. If it runs towards a snag or a rapid, stop it by braking the reel-drum increasingly hard, with high rod point, and then suddenly dropping the rod and letting go the drum. In most cases, the fish will stop when it feels all the pressure gone, and will swim slowly back to its lie.

Until after the fish takes, the rod need not be kept at an angle to the line, because the slipping clutch is an adequate safeguard against any sudden jerk. Even when reeling a fish in, the same thing applies. But whenever the reel drum is being braked with a finger, as when a fish is taking line or being pumped or walked in, the rod point should be kept up at a good angle; the slipping clutch is out of the picture then, and one is apt to let the drum go only after the jerk begins—which, unless the rod top is held up to take the extra strain, is generally too late.

Some exception to the use of very fine gear must be made in fishing large water. Where the stream is wide and heavy enough, even in summer conditions, to put considerable weight in the belly of the line, then something thicker than 2X is called for. From a 5¼-lb. breaking strain it is safer to move up to, say, 8 lb. Some fishermen declare that 10 lb. should be the minimum. I should say it depends on the water. Norway is not Scotland, nor Scotland Devon. Fish as fine as the water allows!

CHAPTER XVII

ROVING A PRAWN

The Prawn's the thing to please the King!

To many fishermen prawning must bring memories of Ireland and of the Irish life, freer than anything else on this earth, which was lived there long ago and now shows signs of returning again, in a more penurious and perhaps a less inconsiderate form, to that delectable country. Can't you see Patsy standing on a ledge half-way down the "lep", his eyes intent on certain shadows ten feet below the creaming surface of the run and on the prawn that you are trying to work down to them? His arms move with the agitation proper to a Manchester bookmaker on St. Leger day or an Edinburgh policeman on point duty. To right or left you move your rod, in desperate interpretation. He is getting all the fun of this. Your turn will come though.

"He has it!" The whispered words do not reach you, but the upraised hands and the sheer beseeching power in the whole attitude would stop even a Hitler from striking too soon. Three seconds pass! Four!—While the twitches come up the line into your very soul. Then Patsy prostrates himself towards you like a muezzin towards the Holy City; up goes your rod; bang go the hooks, solidly, into the fish; out it jumps, all silver and gleaming in the darksome cleft; for an instant Patsy, yourself, the fish are carved motionless on the tablets of Eternity; then the great salmon goes down in a swathe of spray, and the tableau dissolves into goat-like activity.

It is not to Ireland, however, that memory takes me when I think of prawning for salmon, but to a certain part of Dartmoor where, I am bound to say, life was lived on very similar lines. Dart salmon will take a prawn when they will take nothing else. I remember one hardy sportsman, who, after killing five salmon one wild spring day, accepted a bet of five pounds after dinner that he would not round off the half-dozen. He started off on a bicycle at 10 P.M., in pitch darkness, to the river, the weather by that time having stiffened to a sort of blizzard, and—somehow—killed his sixth fish. He declared that he had used a prawn, but someone was churlish enough to suggest that he must have had a good deal of lead on it!

Another fisherman hooked a salmon, much to his surprise, in dead low water while dangling a prawn over the upstream side of Hexworthy Bridge. The water was as clear as gin, and we could see the salmon come up from beneath the bridge as coolly as a minnow and take the prawn before my friend could quite decide whether he wanted it taken or not. However, he tightened more or less automatically, and the salmon, as soon as it felt the hook, rushed down through the arch at the rate of knots, and, although the fisherman tore line off the reel to try and stop it, the drag was still enough to induce it to keep going. Eventually the fisherman cast himself over the parapet into 8 feet of water, rod and all, with a crash that should have stunned every fish in the pool, floated down to the shallows, and, finding that by some miracle his line was still intact, proceeded to land his fish!

The Dart is a short, fast river and rarely remains in good fly order for more than a day or two at a time, so that, in summer months especially, one was compelled to fish with a prawn. I say "compelled" advisedly, because I think that a prawn should be used only after both fly and spinning baits have been tried and proved useless. There is no doubt whatever that a prawn will at times, for some unknown reason, scare salmon nearly to death. I have myself seen a party of salmon in the tail of a pool scatter at the approach of the prawn as though the Muckle Black Silkie himself were after them, and start rushing about the pool in every direction in what to all appearance was a state of absolute panic. Yet at times they will go for a prawn as though they had been waiting all their lives for it.

Is the salmon thinking sometimes of its sea life and of the fact that prawns are just obvious things to eat, and at other times of its childhood where, of course, prawns did not belong, or where a crayfish was a nightmare? Possibly. I do not know, and have not heard, so far, of anyone who does. Whenever a prawn is seen to scare salmon in this way, it is best to pack up at once and change to something else, as it is a mood which is usually not confined to one salmon or even to one pool. It is a sympathetic affection, and looks almost as if it depended on some special element in the weather, which so far nobody has succeeded in discovering.

It is partly for this reason, and partly for the reason that a prawn in the hands of the unclean and wicked is a most useful cover for a 10-0 snatch-hook and a lump of lead, that prawning is often regarded as not a very nice way of taking salmon. But, fairly fished, it is a delightful business. I know of nothing more exciting than the twitch of the gossamer line which tells that somewhere beneath the turmoil of the run a salmon of unknown dimensions is mouthing your bait.

Prawning is essentially a low-water method for use when the fly has failed. There are several ways of working it, all demanding the same fine tackle. Spinning a baby prawn or a shrimp has been described in the chapter on Spinning in Low Water. The same light spinning outfit is ideal for the other methods as well, since they all demand delicate control, often at long distances.

The essence of using a prawn purely as a "still" bait and not as a spinner is to keep it near the bottom and to make it move slowly, so that it behaves as nearly like the "real Mackay" as possible.

The colour of a prawn does not seem to matter. Boiled and fresh prawns do equally well, and Eric Taverner, writing in the Lonsdale Library, has recorded an instance of salmon taking, in very clear water, "old and bleached baits dipped in magenta aniline dye". The effluvia—or whatever corresponds to the thing we call smell—is much more important. Formalin is a bad preserving medium for this reason. Prawns, either fresh or boiled, can be kept for a few days in salt in an *open* jar or tin, and make much more attractive baits than those which have been kept in formalin.

For preserving prawns indefinitely, put them in an airtight glass jar, filled with glycerine or with a strong solution of sugar and water. An idea which Wanless describes in his book, *The Science of Spinning for Salmon and Trout*, of preserving prawns in carbonic acid gas sounds excellent. I have not tried this method but it was designed with the special purpose of obviating smell and keeping the baits clean, and is simplicity itself. Simply put a few spoonfuls of baking powder in the bottom of an airtight jar; pour a little acetic acid on it; test, with a lighted match, the height to which the heavy carbonic acid gas rises as it displaces the air, and when the match goes out just below the lip of the jar place the prawns inside on a little raised shelf of wood or tin, high enough to keep them clear of the acid, and put the lid on the jar.

The prawns for the day's fishing should be mixed with a little salt and carried in a tin in one's pocket. It saves time and trouble in prawning, as it does in every other kind of bait fishing, where mounting the baits is a lengthy and delicate business, if several baits are mounted before setting out.

Standard prawn tackles often suffer from the usual defect of spinning tackles—hooks which are too many and too large. A salmon takes a prawn much more deliberately than it takes a rapidly-spinning bait. The inspection of a prawn lasts longer, and presumably a bristling array of hooks does not conduce to its success. In spinning, too, the salmon has no chance of spitting the bait out when once he has been induced to take it. The line being always fairly taut, any check in the bait's progress is instantly noticeable, and one can tighten at once and round off the work already begun by the current in pulling in the hooks. In prawning, on the other hand, it is not possible to keep in such close touch with the bait. A salmon has much more chance of playing with it, unknown to the fisherman. Often it does this so gently that even a fairly tight line does not record what is happening, and so it is important that the salmon should feel as little of the hooks as possible until it actually makes off with the bait and shows the fisherman that the time has come to strike.

A single hook, one treble, or one or two doubles therefore constitute the best prawn tackles. One should not have a greater number of points than four. The tackle can be arranged in a myriad ways. A pin of some sort is necessary to keep the body of the prawn straight, and this can be either loose, or sliding on the gut, or lashed to a hook, and it can point either up or down. The chief consideration, to my mind, next always to neatness and hooking power, is that the prawn should be easy to put on. A baiting-needle is a thing I detest, and, in view of the present multiplicity of choice, to use a tackle that needs one is, to my mind, like washing was to that of the intelligent small boy, a work of supererogation.

The simplest and neatest rig I have met is the "bayonet" tackle, so-called because it consists simply of a pin shaped like a bayonet and whipped to an eyed hook, to which is attached a short piece of twisted wire

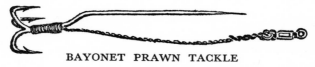

BAYONET PRAWN TACKLE

having a swivel at its upper end. The pin points upwards, and is pushed up from head to tail of the prawn; the hook, which can be single, double, or treble, then lies snugly hidden in the prawn's whiskers. Double a piece of very fine copper wire round the prawn's tail, lash the tail tightly to the twisted wire which forms the backbone of the tackle, and then pass the two ends of the copper wire diagonally round both prawn and tackle wire in a criss-cross lashing till they reach the head, when they are made fast by being twisted together. Weight can be added if necessary by winding lead wire round the wire of the tackle before the latter is tied in. The hook with its pin can be attached to a piece of heavy gut instead of to wire, but there is no point in using gut, as wire is much more hard-wearing, and, in this position—close against the underside of the prawn—just as little visible.

The advantage of this upturned-pin tackle, besides its neatness and simplicity, is that the prawn is constantly supported by the pin in its passage through the water, and does not tend to slip down, as it often does when mounted on a downturned-pin tackle, where it has to rely entirely on the hooks for support. An extra single hook or flat double can be whipped in half-way up the wire, so as to lie close to the underside of the prawn without making the total armament much more noticeable. But all hooks must—forgive me if I repeat this *ad nauseam*, it is so very important—be as sharp as needles. You will be using fine tackle and often striking from a long distance, and it is absolutely necessary that the hooks should penetrate easily.

Always use a swivel at the head of the flight when prawning. A prawn rolls a good deal and will soon put turns into a trace that has no swivel in it. If a nylon monofilament line is being used, the trace need be only a short length of nylon, rather weaker than the line. At or near the joint put any lead that may be necessary, in the form of twists of lead wire tied on with thread, or large split shot pinched on to a piece of thread and tied on, the thread in either case being weaker than the trace, so that if the lead hangs up on the bottom it will carry away without the trace being broken. Never pinch a split shot on to the trace or line. It not only weakens the gut but is quite impossible to take off again. If you must put lead on to the trace itself, use Simplex leads, which are so shaped that they can be made fast by a very gentle pressure and easily levered open again with a thumb nail.

I don't like lead on the prawn tackle or in the body of the prawn unless I have to cast into a stiff head wind and the prawn shows a tendency to double back and foul the line. I would rather see the lead about 18 inches up the trace. The reason is that you can only tell if the prawn is fishing deep enough by feeling an occasional bump as it trips over a stone. If much lead is put on the prawn itself your hook points will soon be blunted, if not broken. Moreover, the prawn will "lean", as it is drawn through the water, at a most unnatural angle. If the lead is on the trace the lead itself will take many of the bumps and at the same time keep the prawn level.

The choice of fishing tactics will depend on the anatomy of the pool. If it has a heavy stickle at its head, salmon will lie, if the weather is hot and the water low, right in the white water in the stickle's throat. Begin here by making a short cast square across to the near edge of the surges. Let the prawn sink, and, when you feel it trip on the stones, bring it back by taking in the line in slow draws, about a foot at a time. Make the next cast further, and higher up, even into the tail of the pool above, if necessary, so as to make sure that in this faster water the prawn will have reached the bottom by the time it gets abreast of you. Perhaps the line will stop and sweep into a bow, and there will come up it an electric twitch which tells of a fish mouthing the bait.

Opinion is divided as to what one should do when this happens. Some fishermen advocate striking at once, and Taverner mentions watching a salmon take his prawn in clear water, and giving the salmon a slack line as an experiment, with the result that it played with the prawn for a moment and then spat it out with great determination. As a general rule, then, I do not think that it pays to strike too hurriedly. So often a salmon seems merely to stop the prawn with its nose or nibble at it in a suspicious sort of way before it decides to take hold. To strike at the preliminary twitches rarely results in hooking the fish. I always like to wait until the line moves off—I can be sure then that the fish has the prawn in its mouth.

When you have fished out the throat of the stickle, wade out as far as you can and cast across and down. In the fast water the only way to sink the prawn was to cast it well upstream; now it will sink, whatever the angle, but casting down will make it come round more slowly. Keep it on the bottom by giving line if necessary. If the current is still too fast, add more lead to the trace. If it checks too much on the bottom, hold the line by a finger on the drum of the reel and let the current lift it. Let the prawn come round to the dangle, then work it up towards you along the near edge of the stickle in slow even jerks.

When the water is low and clear one should use as little lead as possible, and if it is found difficult to keep the prawn down when casting across the current it pays to stand as near as possible to the head of the stickle and let the prawn away down it, keeping the rod low. The prawn can be made to travel more slowly and deeply by this method than by any other.

Before fishing the stickle do not neglect the smooth "hang" at the foot of the pool above. Get well above it, cast down and across, and let the prawn come round just where the water gathers speed to plunge into the first of the surges.

In deep pots, such as are common in a steep granite-bedded river such as the Dart, where a solid fall smashes down into a deep, seething hole, a sort of sink-and-draw method often pays. Drop the prawn in and let it shuffle about on the bottom until the salmon have had a good look at it. Then, if nothing happens, draw it up quite slowly almost to the surface and let it sink again. This will often bring up a salmon.

It is difficult, with the ordinary light spinning outfit, to work a prawn properly amongst big scattered rocks. If there is any stream, such a place is probably an excellent fishing ground, but in trying to get the prawn down behind some distant boulder the line sinks and fouls an intermediate one. If there is a fair depth of water a float is the best solution of this problem. The rod must be as long as the interval between float and prawn, that is to say, as long as the water is deep.

If a fairly long rod—say a 14-foot—is used with a light nylon line, the line between the rod and the float can be kept clear of the water even when the float is a considerable distance away. And it *must* be kept clear of the water—or, at any rate, kept from sinking—as any drowned line between the rod and the float not only puts the float out of control but also defeats its main object, which is to enable you to fish the prawn at the proper depth on the far side of obstacles. The only alternative to the light nylon line is a light floating plastic or greased silk line. The float can be a large cork, or a couple of corks, with a feather stuck to it to make it more visible.

A float is an extremely neat way both of circumventing obstacles and of hanging a prawn in a lie. The cast can be made above and beyond the lie and use made of the current to manœuvre the float and prawn into it. The float tells just where the prawn is. When the prawn has been in the first lie long enough, it can be brought over in turn into other lies nearer your own bank without any necessity for making a fresh cast.

CHAPTER XVIII

WORMING

> And now I shall tell you, that which may be called a secret:
> I have been a fishing with old *Oliver Henly* (now with God) a
> noted Fisher, both for *Trout* and *Salmon*, and have observed that
> he would usually take three or four worms out of his bag and
> put them into a little box in his pocket, where he would usually
> let them continue half an hour or more, before he would bait his
> hook with them; I have ask'd him his reason, and he has re-
> plied. *He did but pick the best out to be in a readiness against he baited*
> *his hook the next time*: But he has been observed both by other,
> and my self, to catch more fish than I or any other body, that
> has ever gone a fishing with him, could do, especially *Salmons*;
> and I have been told lately by one of his most intimate and
> secret friends, that the box in which he put those worms was
> anointed with a drop, or two, or three of the Oil of *Ivy-berries*,
> made by expression or infusion, and that by the wormes re-
> maining in that box an hour, or a like time, they had incor-
> porated a kind of smel that was irresistibly attractive, enough
> to force any fish, within the smel of them, to bite. This I heard
> not long since from a friend, but have not tryed it.
>
> *The Compleat Angler*

In extreme youth it was one of my less arduous but
more objectionable tasks to supply worms to any
member of my family who happened to want to fish.
The worms had to be forthcoming without any delay,
and there was a row if they were not both clean and
tough. After a time I started a "wormery" in an immense old flower-pot, filled with cool sphagnum moss,
from which anyone wanting worms could go and take
them without bothering me, and which I could re-
plenish at leisure on days appointed by myself for the
purpose.

However, as one might have guessed, this innocent
and convenient arrangement proved only an incitement
to fresh tyranny. This time it was the *size* of the worms
I provided which was called in question. Some, it
appeared, were too large for trout and yet much too
small for salmon; and accordingly I was directed to set
up a separate establishment for each of the two sizes
required. I remember being accompanied, as I made
the rounds of my various worming grounds, by a com-
mittee of mighty fishers and receiving instruction as to
exactly how long and how wide a worm must be before
it could be considered capable of catching a salmon.
It had to be a perfect serpent, they said—the sort of
worm, in fact, that I had previously been in the habit
of leaving severely alone in case it should turn and
bite me.

I took it all in, being very young and desirous of
becoming one day a mighty fisher myself, filled with
truth and wisdom. And in fullness of time (though long
after my illusions as to this class of being had vanished)
I learnt that a large worm is no better for catching
salmon than a small one.

The validity of the flower-pot and the sphagnum
moss, however, remained. I used to put shards on the
hole in the bottom of the pot to stop the worms escaping, an occasional drop of milk on the top, and turn
the whole contents of the pot upside down about once
in three days so that the worms should work down
through the moss to the bottom again, cleaning and
toughening themselves on the way. I do not know
where this lore had been acquired—I certainly didn't
invent it—but it is all sound doctrine and to this day
I flatter myself that, in those high and far-off times, I
produced a very fine class of worm.

As to whether worming for salmon is sporting or

unsporting, it is unnecessary to enter into any prolonged discussion. I suppose the test whether a way of fishing is sporting or unsporting must be that applied in assessing any other kind of conduct; namely, whether or not it hurts other people. But, before leaving this question, I should just like to describe the most success-ful, appropriate and innocuous piece of fishing I ever witnessed. While sailing one summer in Norway, I saw a local inhabitant fishing in the torrent that comes down from the Bondhusbrae glacier above the Sundal hamlet at the head of Mauranger. He was fishing in a sort of green maelstrom with a piece of thick bamboo about 12 feet long, from which depended a piece of strong brass wire ending in a thing like a small octopus, which I found later was a large leaded hook well smothered with worms. By his side lay two small salmon, one of about 6 lb., the other about 8 lb. In front of the rock on which he stood was perhaps 10 square yards of streaming, tossing backwash, through which a bait could, I suppose, be got to the bottom. The rest of the torrent was a roaring green-and-white mass, so cold that a band of vapour, quite distinct from the spray, lay above the rocks and birches through which it fell.

As I watched him moving his pole about over the backwash, it suddenly jagged down and the "line" shot out into the white water. The fisherman got both hands to his pole, braced himself in the manner of a tunny fisherman, gave a mighty heave, and brought a salmon out of the smother like a cork out of a bottle. I wished I had had more Norwegian with which to compliment him. It may not have been a noble sight, but to catch a salmon at all in such a place was an achievement, and he was certainly doing no harm to anybody.

There are many places in English and Scottish as

well as Norwegian rivers where a worm or a prawn
is the only bait that can possibly be brought within
sight of the salmon; though conditions in the British
Isles are rarely so hectic as to compel the use of such
unbreakable tackle as that which my Norwegian friend
was using. There is a state of the river, too, in which a
worm is the only way to take a fish, and that is when
the water is so thick that the salmon cannot see a bait
and the fisherman has to appeal to its sense of smell.
Should one leave the river alone when it is in such a
state? Perhaps one would, if one had the time and
opportunity to wait for better conditions, but if time is
short and opportunity is rare, then I see no reason why
one should not try for a salmon in the only possible
way. One is, after all, fishing "with one rod and
line only" (as the licence clause so often runs), which
effectually dispels any fear of over-fishing the river,
and, provided one does not fish with tackle heavier
than the situation demands, one must use as much skill
in the play of a salmon hooked with a worm as is
needed when playing a fish hooked with a fly or
spinner.

The stationary-drum reel and nylon line have
increased the artistry in worm fishing, just as they
have increased it in spinning and prawning. Before its
advent, worming was certainly a clumsy business. A
worm, or even a bunch of worms, was too heavy and
fragile to cast with a fly rod and too light to cast from
a spinning reel, so that the tactics of worming were
restricted to "dapping" and swinging the worm with a
line not much longer than the rod. The long rod which
one was thus compelled to use was handy in a small
rocky river like the Dart, where the bait had to be
reached into small holes and kept clear of boulders;
but in any larger, less obstructed, water one was sadly

hampered by having to fish all the time with the bait practically under the rod point.

With a light thread-line outfit, however, a worm can be cast 20 yards or more, and so made to cover lies which were previously far out of reach. It also enables a far more sensitive and accurate control to be exercised in working the bait. More than this, the extra range of cast and fineness of tackle make it possible to worm for salmon in low clear water. A worm is a safer bait than a prawn under such conditions, as it does not frighten the fish.

The time-honoured tackle for worming is the single hook, and it is still difficult to find anything more efficient. It holds the worms together better than any multiple-hook tackle; it can be completely hidden; and, owing to the metal being covered by worms, it is a long time before the salmon feels it. A No. 4 round-bend hook is the most convenient in size and shape. Three 3-inch worms will more than cover it, if the hook is threaded through the middle inch of each one in turn. The two-hook tackle, in which each of two No. 6 or No. 8 hooks is tied to a separate short piece of gut attached to the end of the trace, so that the hooks hang level, back to back, is also excellent. Each hook can be covered properly with worms, and their being close together and yet free to move past each other greatly assists their chances of hooking.

SINGLE HOOK, BAITED

TWO-HOOK WORM TACKLE

I do not like either the Pennell or the Stewart tackles. The hooks cannot be hidden, and the fish feels them much sooner than it does a single hook; I do not believe they hook any better than a single, and they have to be constantly rebaited; if a fish touches the worm, the worm invariably breaks, leaving its two ends on separate hooks and a hiatus in the middle, which can only be remedied by taking the fragments off and putting on a fresh worm.

It facilitates repairs to use only eyed hooks. A whipped hook makes it easier to thread the worm up past the shank, and allows a bristle to be whipped in, point upwards, to keep the worm from slipping down; but it is really very little more difficult to thread a worm past an eyed hook, and the effect of the bristle can be gained by tying the hook on with a Turle knot and leaving an end of gut, a quarter of an inch long, pointing upwards from the knot.

The trace for worming is the same as that used for prawning. It need be only 18 inches long, weaker than the line, with a tiny swivel at its upper end. Only a very small amount of lead is needed, and it can consist either of Simplex-shaped leads, pressed gently on to the end of the trace above the swivel, or of shot, or lead wire. If lead wire or swan shot are used, they should be tied to the upper eye of the swivel with a piece of weak cotton, in accordance with the principle that it is better to lose the lead than to lose the trace.

Worming for salmon is very like roving a prawn. The main difference is that the worms should never be made to move against the current. The lead on the trace should constantly be felt bumping the bottom, and the bait should be allowed to travel at current speed and no faster. In heavy water, fish in a place where the water is of medium depth and provides an obvious ease. The thin fringe of a stickle—well clear of the main weight of water—the shallower eddies, any rock-lies where the wash is not too strong, and—in level reaches and pool tails—the water close under the bank, are all good places to try.

In low clear water, the identical places that one fishes with a prawn are also the best for a worm. Perhaps a little more attention could be paid to quieter water. The tail of a pool, well studded with rocks, which is the first quiet water above a long stretch of rough, will hold salmon even in hot weather. They will stop there for a breather, and may often be persuaded to take a worm, especially if the surface is well ruffled by wind. Any cleft or other narrow place, in which there is a fair current, is also good for a worm, no matter how deep the water is. The same applies to any stream running past cliffs or shelves of rock. The great advantage of a worm is that it can be made to search places that could not be reached with a fly or spinner.

A salmon rarely takes a worm with a bang, in the way that it so often takes a prawn. Probably it knows that the worm cannot dart away as a prawn can. And so a gentle checking of the line is usually the first indication one has that "something is up". The way to discover exactly what is happening is to keep the line always across the forefinger of the spare hand. This will soon become so sensitive as to enable you to distinguish at once between the dull thrumming of the current, which indicates a snag, and the "electric" twitches, however tiny, which tell of a salmon chewing the bait.

A salmon is apt to play with a bunch of worms just as it plays with a prawn, and so one should wait before striking, until some decided movement of the line shows that the fish has taken the bait into its mouth.

CHAPTER XIX

SALMON IN LAKES

O weel may the boatie row
That fills a heavy creel.
JOHN EWEN

LOCAL knowledge is what really counts when fishing
for salmon in lakes. While local knowledge is useful for
fishing in rivers, it is absolutely necessary when fishing
in a lake. In a river, at least, even though you do not
know exactly where the salmon are, you can generally
say that they are within 20 or 30 yards of you, and
there are few beats that cannot be covered entirely in
the course of the day by diligent fishing. In a lake, on
the other hand, you might fish for a month and only
cover one small corner of it; and there is very little to
tell you that that corner is not the wrong one.

Failing the local fisherman or gillie, who can put you
at once on to the places where salmon lie, almost the
only means of discovering where to fish is your own
long and painfully-gathered experience. There are,
however, a few broad rules which may help to hasten
the process. The first place that should receive attention is the area near the principal outfall of the lake.
If there are any salmon in the lake at all, this is the
way they have come and the way that others will follow
them. They find in the quiet water of the lake a wel-
come respite after the journey up the river and generally rest for a time in the first part of it they come to.
If there are any large boulders in the area near the

outfall, salmon will almost certainly be found resting near them, especially when the level of the water in the lake is higher than usual, because that is the time when the river below will be high also and salmon will be running up it.

Next in importance as a hunting-ground are the infalls of any rivers up which salmon are known to run. Salmon are most likely to be found in these places when the rivers above are low, because then the fish are prevented from running up by lack of water, and congregate in increasing numbers until the next spate lets them go on. When these upper rivers are swollen the outfalls will be tenantless and it is generally useless to fish them, because any new arrivals will probably run straight up into the rivers without stopping to rest.

The lies that are far distant from the rivers can only be discovered by local knowledge or experience. Generally speaking, salmon are more likely to be found somewhere near a line drawn between the principal infall and the principal outfall and in depths between 6 and 20 feet than they are elsewhere. Apart from that, it is impossible to lay down any rules for finding them. It is often worth fishing round a big submerged rock, especially where there are several such rocks close together; also off rocky points, in small deep bays, and near any sunken fence that runs out into deep water. But there are so many of these features in any big lake as to make this much too vague a direction. Really the only thing to do is ask the local fishermen—and preferably two or three of them, *privatim et seriatim*—where the fish are likely to be found. And if they seem in any doubt about it—hire them! One needs a boat in any case, and it is a pity if the boatman cannot find a fish for you.

Salmon can be caught in a lake with either a fly or a spinner, although there are few lakes in which a fly is really of much use. Of these, Loch Lomond is probably the best known. There, a fly is used a good deal in the summer for both salmon and sea trout, being fished with a strong single-handed rod, very much as a string of wet flies is fished for trout. The boat is allowed to drift across likely places and the fly thrown and allowed to sink a little before being drawn back. In several of the Irish lakes, salmon are occasionally caught with a May-fly fished on a blowline.

Spinning for salmon in a lake is usually the dull business known as trolling, where you sit in a boat, your rod stuck out over the stern, and get colder and colder while the boatman rows the boat about with your bait trailing behind. A stone is laid on the line between the first ring and the reel, of such a weight that a fish taking a bait will be hooked properly without breaking the trace. Placing the stone accurately on the line, seeing that the proper length of line is let out, and occasionally taking it in and removing pieces of weed from the flight, constitute, as far as the fisherman is concerned, the whole art and science of trolling. The boatman is the only member of the party who has a chance of using either his brain or his muscles.

Apart from its being both cold and dull, trolling is not, to my mind, the most effective way of fishing a spinning bait in a lake. It is necessary, of course, to fish from a boat, since much of the water cannot be covered from the bank; but we know that a boat disturbs salmon, and, in trolling, the boat passes first over every salmon to which the bait is offered. A much better and more interesting way of fishing from a boat is to let it drift, while you stand up in it and cast the bait repeatedly at right angles to its course. The advantages of this way of doing things are:

(1) The fisherman is not cold, or at any rate is less

cold than he would be if he sat still. (2) He has no opportunity of becoming comatose, but, on the contrary, is using his wits to a certain extent in casting and drawing back the bait, and so is always ready for a fish when it comes along. (3) The boat is not rowed, but drifts, and so makes less disturbance. (4) The boat does not act as outrider to the bait, warning everything that sees it to clear out of the way. (5) A small patch of good water, *e.g.* the mouths or intakes of rivers, can be fished thoroughly without frightening the fish; the small splash of a bait attracts fish, where a boat only scares them. (6) A greater variety of water can be covered, because a bait can be thrown into places where a boat could not be rowed—amongst rocks, for instance, or across patches of weeds.

Cast, where possible, *into* the deeper water *from* the shallower water, so that the slope of the bottom conforms with the slanting path of the bait as it is drawn up towards the boat. Let the bait sink well before starting to bring it home, and let it fish to the bottom.

It is something of a paradox that, although the approach of a boat frightens the salmon, the salmon, when it is hooked, will often take station immediately beneath the boat and keep pace exactly with it, so that the fisherman frequently gets the impression that his line is hung up on the keel. Probably the fish imagines that the boat, which was probably allowed to drift quietly as soon as it took hold, is some kind of rock or shelter, and this idea may be heightened by the fact that it is impossible to exert a heavy strain on a fish when it is immediately underneath one's feet. If it will not move, rout it out with a gaff handle. Do not use an oar, for the edges of the blade are probably worn, and there are both splinters and metal bands on it in which the trace may catch and break.

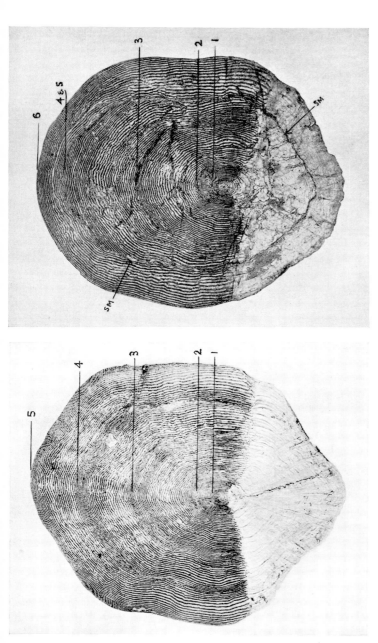

CLUES TO THE PAST

Photomicrographs of salmon scales.

Left: A maiden large spring cock fish from the *Wye*, weight 27 lb., length 42 inches, girth 21 inches; 2 years of river life and 3 years feeding in the sea; 5 years old.

Right: A previously-spawned female fish from the *Wye*, weight 26 lb., length 38 inches, girth 21½ inches; 2 years of river life and about 2½ years feeding in the sea, followed by several months in the river before spawning. Outside the spawning mark the rings show a further full year's growth in salt water; 6 years old.

SOME BIG ONES

Top: A 35-pounder from the Wye.
Bottom: A 47½-pounder and a 45-pounder, both from Norway.

Rather more line will be needed for playing a salmon in a lake than is needed in a river. The usual trick for stopping a fish—a strong pressure, followed by a sudden release—does not always work in a lake, for, although the fish may think itself free, there is seldom any obvious shelter near at hand to induce it to stop. The chances are that it will just swim on aimlessly until the line comes taut again, when, of course, it once more rushes off. Since the tackle for fishing the still water of a lake must be kept fairly fine, a big fish cannot be stopped by pressure alone; and if it takes it into its head to run straight, it cannot be stopped, even by stratagem, on a length of line which would be ample for fishing a river. Where big fish are expected, have 200 yards of line at least, and be on the safe side.

The only way to acquire a sound knowledge of lake fishing for salmon is to fish the same lake at as many different times of year and states of water and weather as possible, and to make detailed notes of every fish caught. This, of course, is also a great help in gaining experience of a river. But, because the water is so much smaller, salmon in a river are much more easily observed than they are in a lake. One can say in spring that they are in the pool tails, in summer that they are in the streams. But a lake has such a vast and expressionless countenance that it is only by noting down every possible hint, in the shape of the details of each capture, that one can ever attain to an idea of what goes on beneath it.

The bait, the time of day, the weather, and the temperatures both of air and water are, of course, as important circumstances in the capture of a lake fish as they are in that of a river fish. But it is more important still, when a fish is caught in a lake, to note the condition at that time of the rivers that enter and leave the lake, the *depth*, as nearly as you can judge, at which the bait or fly was being fished, the *height* of the water, and the exact place where the fish took hold.

The height of water in the lake cannot be spotted at once as it can in a river. One cannot, merely by looking at the lake, say that it is "in good order". The only way to find out whether it is "high" or "low" is to refer to some kind of gauge. A height gauge can easily be made by driving a post, marked in feet and inches, into the bed of the lake at any place where the water is about 3 feet deep; 3 feet is usually a sufficient depth, for the water level is unlikely to go down more than this. It does not matter in the least where the scale cuts the surface to begin with, so long as there is a couple of feet of the scale both above and below water. You do not need to know what is the actual average depth of the lake at that particular point. What you do want to know is *how much* the lake rises or falls from one day to the next. The place on the scale which cuts the surface on the first day can be taken as the normal. Suppose it is 2 feet 1 inch. Perhaps that reading remains constant for a week and you catch no fish, and then it rains hard for two days, and on the third day you catch several fish and find that the scale is reading 2 feet 3 inches. That shows you that the lake has gone up 2 inches in those two days and that it is that 2 inches which may have had some bearing on your success. The scale tells you the *difference* in level from day to day and from week to week, and that is what you need to know.

The exact place where the fish was hooked can usually be identified by reference to some point or bay in the shore line, but where there is no conspicuous feature of this kind, one should try to fix the spot by taking a pair of bearings. A cottage and a hill-top, for instance, in line in one direction, and perhaps a couple of conspicuous trees on an island in line in another direction, should be noted carefully. You will then be able, on any future occasion, by referring to these marks and getting them in line again, to put yourself in exactly the same position.

CHAPTER XX

BIOGRAPHY

... the one most worthy to be protected is that worthy
gentleman salmon, who is generous enough to go down to the
sea weighing five ounces, and to come back next year weighing
five pounds, without having cost the soil or the state one
farthing.
                                          CHARLES KINGSLEY

THE object of the salmon's long and arduous journey
up the river is to find a place where its eggs will be as
little damaged as possible by foul water and floods. The
water is generally cleanest and most constant in flow at
the very source of the river, where it wells out of the
hillside in clear, cool springs; and the salmon therefore
goes as far up the river as it can before depositing its
eggs. It is quite extraordinary into what shallow water
a salmon will go at spawning time. It was my good
fortune to live for some years on the upper waters of
the West Dart, and each autumn the great fish would
appear in tiny stickles which were scarcely deep
enough to cover them. Sometimes during a dry October
they would be virtually imprisoned in a shrunken pool.
I have often seen a salmon, that was being chased by
another, miss the narrow exit, and roll clear out of
water over a broad strip of gravel between one shallow
and the next.

The changes that take place in the shape and condition of the salmon—especially of the cock fish—during the journey up the river, are almost unbelievable.
The feeding teeth with which it was equipped while

it was in the sea drop out shortly before it enters the river, and in their place grows a new set of teeth, even larger and broader, which Dr. Tchernavin has termed "breeding" teeth. In the male, the bones in the jaws lengthen considerably, the forward part of the skull falls in and becomes concave instead of convex, and at the end of the lower jaw grows up a bill or hook of cartilage, which is sometimes very large and gives the spawning male such a distinctive appearance. There is apparently little purpose in these changes. The salmon does not feed with its breeding teeth. They may possibly help the male in fighting, for it fights by catching hold of its opponent, not by butting it with the hook on its jaw. After spawning is over, the skull gradually reverts to its normal shape, the breeding teeth eventually drop out, and the hook on the jaw of the male is absorbed.

For depositing their eggs the salmon choose a place where a fair current flows evenly over a bed of gravel or small stones. The female makes the redd by violent contortions of the body. These contortions disturb the gravel beneath the fish, and this disturbed gravel is washed by the current into a heap. The eggs are actually shed while the female is lying quite still in the redd and they are washed into the interstices of the gravel heap, which protects them, more or less, during the period of incubation. It is now generally agreed that this heap of gravel, or "redd" as it is called, is not consciously manufactured by the fish. It is formed incidentally by the violent movements of the female fish in spawning. Contrary to the old belief, the hook on the jaw of the male is not used for digging out the redd. Nor does the male take any part in the formation of the redd, for it ranges alongside the female and drops its milt on to the newly extruded eggs without any violent movement. The only gravel disturbed by the male is the small amount which may be displaced while the fish is fighting with, or chasing, other males.

The eggs, when extruded, are pink and translucent, but they turn to a milky opaqueness when fertilised by contact with the milt. The incubation period is between ninety and one hundred and sixty days, according to the temperature of the water. The alevin lives, for the first fifty days after it hatches out, on the nourishment in the umbilical sac, which hangs down from its throat. As this food is absorbed, the sac gradually disappears, and the young fish begins to forage for itself. The mortality amongst eggs and alevins is very small, but among fry just beginning to feed is believed to be terrific. About one egg in a thousand becomes a grown salmon.

In their first summer the little fish are known as parr, and it is to prevent their being mistaken at this stage for trout that Fishery Boards often put up notices near the river which include a diagram to show the difference between the two fish. It is said that a parr slaps its head with its tail when it is lifted out of the water, whereas a trout cannot do this; but a more certain distinction can be made by looking at the maxillary bones and the fins. The maxillary bones are the two paddle-shaped bones that slant backwards, one on either side of the upper jaw. In the parr, these extend only level with the middle of the eye; in the trout they extend as far as the hinder edge of the eye or even beyond it. The adipose fin of the parr—the little embryo fin on the underside of the fish, next its tail—is a pale whitish colour; in the trout it is red or orange.

When the feed in the river is exceptionally poor, the parr may remain there as long as five years, but the majority of them work down to the sea during their third or fourth spring. They then put on a silvery sheen which obscures the dark finger-like markings that made them look so like young trout, and become known as smolts. Most of them are then between 4 and 6 inches long.

Apparently only about 5 per cent of smolts ever return from the sea. Very little is known about their sea life, except that they grow very fast owing to the rich feeding that comes their way. Autopsies of young salmon netted near the mouths of rivers have shown that their diet consists largely of herring, but that they also eat sand-eels, shrimps, prawns, whiting, haddock, and many other kinds of marine creatures, so that it is impossible to tell exactly where they go in their search for food.

They may return to the river at any time between one and five or more years after they have left it. This much we can now definitely ascertain by "reading" the scales of the fish—a science which was evolved by Mr H. W. Johnston, Mr Arthur Hutton, and others. When examined under the microscope, the undersides of the scales of the salmon show a number of ridges, like the rings of a tree, which have been found to bear an exact relation to the life and the growth of the fish. Those that are near together indicate a period of slow growth in the river; those that are more widely spaced show a period of faster growth in the sea; while a ragged break in the sequence shows the loss of weight and condition, the stationary or retrograde period, during spawning. Salmon always try to return to the river which they left to go to sea as has been proved by smolt marking in Scotland, Norway, and elsewhere. This holds good also with the fry hatched from eggs which have been transferred from one river to another. No doubt cases occur when for some reason, such as a block

15

in the stream, salmon are unable to get up it, in which case it is assumed that they ascend another stream close by, but the general law is now so well established that there is no longer any real doubt about it.

"Grilse" is the name given to salmon which return to the river during the year following that in which they left it. The heaviest recorded weight of a grilse is 14 lb. The salmon that return after two years, *i.e.* during the spring of the second year after they left the river, weigh up to about 15 lb., and are known as small spring fish. "Small summer fish" are those that return during the summer of their second year's absence, and they may weigh 10 lb. more than the small springers, owing to the increase in the amount of marine food as summer advances. Salmon returning in the spring and summer of later years are respectively termed "large springers" and "large summer fish", and they weigh approximately 9 lb. for every year spent in the sea. The monsters—fish of 40 lb. and upwards, of which a few are taken every year—are salmon which have spent four or more years in the sea.

Salmon have been known to spawn as many as five times, but the great majority spawn only once. Most male salmon die soon after spawning, and of the kelts that do survive to reach the sea, only 10 per cent ever come back a second time, and these form only 2 to 5 per cent of the total run in any one year. A salmon that is on its second or subsequent return to the river can be distinguished from a maiden fish by the spots on the gill-covers and below the lateral line. These spots gave rise to a fish of this class being called on some rivers a "bull trout", and it used to be thought at one time that "bull trout" were a separate species. Occasionally a fish ascends the river without spawning at all. It is then called a "rawner", or a "baggot".

SALMON ASCENDING THE FRASER RIVER, BRITISH COLUMBIA

Where it is only a slight exaggeration to say that one can walk across the river on the backs of salmon, and where the canning factories dredge them out with mechanical scoops! Practically all these fish die in the river.

[Star Photo

OUR FRIENDS FROM THE TIDEWAY

Netsmen on the Tay.

CHAPTER XXI

HOW A RIVER CAN BE IMPROVED

> Deil tak the dirty trading loon
> Wad gar the water ca' his wheel,
> And drift his dyes and poisons doun
> By fair Tweed-side at Ashiesteel!
> ANDREW LANG, *Ballade of the Tweed*

THERE are innumerable ways in which a salmon river can be improved. The mortality among the young fry can be decreased by encouraging the growth of algae in the headwaters and by keeping down natural enemies. Banks can be repaired; trees can be cut back when they interfere with casting, or stances arranged to clear them; snags, brought down by the winter floods, can be dragged out of the water; a path can be constructed wherever the steepness of the bank involves a scramble; and a fishing hut can be installed and furnished. But undoubtedly the most important point of policy is to ensure that a sufficient number of salmon can reach the spawning grounds easily. The means of doing this are to stop pollution, to create artificial resting-places for the fish, to arrange that the nets at the mouth of the river shall be taken off for a sufficient part of every week, and, most important of all, to remove or circumvent difficult obstacles, such as falls and weirs.

All these improvements can be roughly classified under two headings: those which a single owner can make himself, and those which, either from their magnitude or from the generality of their effects, have to be undertaken jointly by the owners of the whole river.

Most of the improvements which are within the compass of the owner of a single beat will tend to enure for the immediate benefit of the fisherman, rather than of the fish. There are, however, a certain number of things that the owner of the beat can do which directly help the fish, as well as the fishing in that particular beat, and the chief of them is the manufacture of lies in which the fish can rest. In most beats even this will not be necessary, for the bed of the river will be sufficiently varied to provide plenty of natural resting-places. It is in a fast, dull, evenly flowing stretch that artificial resting-places are needed.

The most obvious way of making them is to place big boulders in various places in the stream. For a muddy or sandy stream the boulders should be roughly spherical, so that mud or sand is not deposited behind them by too extensive a back-wash. In a granite-bedded river the shape of the boulders is not so important. To be effective, each boulder should be at least 2 feet in diameter; 3 feet is better. A rock of this size sounds an awkward object to handle, but it weighs far less in the water than it does in the air, and much of the difficulty is avoided if the rock is chosen from a place in the river-bed as near as possible to the site for which it is destined. If this is done, the rock need never be lifted out of the water. It can be slung, submerged between two boats, from a stout baulk lashed across the gunwales, and towed to its new position. Failing boulders, concrete blocks make an efficient substitute and can be more easily handled owing to the possibility of moulding a large eye into them, through which a rope can be rove.

The advantage of the boulder-lie is that it is just as

easy to arrange in deep water as it is in shallow. Another way of creating an artificial lie is to build a
"croy"—a sort of jetty running out from the bank—
which deflects the current and leaves a patch of quiet
water in its lee. In deep water a croy is an expensive
undertaking, for it has to be very broad at the base if it
is to stand against floods. But in depths up to 5 or 6 feet
it can be made relatively easily. The most vulnerable
part of the croy is its outer end, and if possible a place
should be chosen where there already exists, at the right
distance from the bank, a large boulder, well bedded
into the floor of the river, which can be used as a
natural anchor. Boulders make the best material for
building the croy, and they should be large ones. It is
only possible to make a lasting job with small stones if
they are enclosed in wire netting of heavy gauge, so as
to make a sort of bolster. But the objection to that is
that any hook touching it will probably catch. Eventually, too, the wire netting will rot and let the stones out.
Concrete is good, but it must be most carefully mixed
and bedded or it will soon split. Fair-sized rough blocks
of concrete are effective and less expensive.

Before it is decided to make a croy, it is important
to try to visualise exactly what the effect will be. The
object is to make an ease downstream of the croy in
which salmon will lie, and perhaps, too, to make a
stance for casting so that the line will clear trees on the
bank. But where the bottom is soft the current may
scour a deep hole off the end of the croy, and under-
mine it, or deposit the excavated material in some good
lie further downstream. And where floods bring down
a lot of mud this may easily be deposited in the quiet
water of the eddy behind the croy, and so fill up
the space and make it useless. Again, if the bank is
soft the eddy may scoop it away. Or if the opposite

bank is soft the current flung over by the croy may damage it.

If the croy is set at a good downstream slant and its inner end built well into the bank, the erosion by the current will be minimised. But where the fishing is held only on one side of the stream it is, in any case, a wise policy to approach the owner of the opposite bank and obtain his goodwill before carrying out the scheme.

The construction of a fish pass, to help the salmon past falls or weirs, is usually too costly an undertaking for a single owner, but, where the beat includes a weir with shallow water under it, a judicious use of dynamite to deepen the take-off below the fall will greatly help salmon to surmount it. As matters generally stand, it is the owner of the beat above the weir who threatens to come down and use dynamite on the weir itself! But a great deal of good could be done with little trouble if the effects of deepening the water under the weir were more widely appreciated. A vertical fall 5 feet high, with shallow water beneath it, will stop all but a very few salmon. Most of them will try to get over it and hurt themselves sorely in the process through falling back on to the rocks beneath or finally becoming exhausted. But a sufficient depth of water immediately under the fall—say 4 to 5 feet—enables them to get up speed for an effective leap. It also prevents the kelts and smolts from damaging themselves as they fall back towards the sea.

Poaching netsmen can be checkmated to a large extent by driving spiles into the beds of pools. Only 6 inches to 1 foot need to be left above the ground— enough to catch the foot-rope of a net—but the spiles must be set in firmly enough to resist the pull of three or four strong men. The top of each spile should be turned over into a hook that points downstream. The heavier gauges of hooked steel bars used in ferro-concrete buildings make excellent spiles.

Where a river is in the hands of a single owner, the salmon can sometimes be helped by an artificial spate, made by damming back the water in the upper reaches and releasing it in times of drought by means of a sluice-gate. This has been done with great success in some of the short rivers in the Hebrides, where several lochs are connected by short links of river with each other and with the sea. The most notable instance was the Grimersta, in which salmon were badly held up by lack of water, and where the creation of artificial spates, carefully timed and regulated, resulted in enormous bags. But it is difficult to arrange, if there are several owners who want to fish at different times.

Beyond making boulder-lies, building croys, deepening the take-off below a weir, and preventing poaching and pollution in his own beat, there is not much that an owner can do by himself to improve the river as a whole. The rest of his single-handed activities will be directed to improving his own particular beat. Here there may be snags to be grappled out; trees that interfere with casting to be cut down; stances for casting to be made—where a croy is not needed, a light jetty made of a flattened pine trunk can often be arranged to give access to a convenient rock—and there are also paths to be cut, banks to be repaired with brushwood fascines, or camp shedding, well backed with stone, and a fishing hut to be established.

A fishing hut is an essential wherever the beat is at all far distant from the house, and its proper furnishing is a matter for some consideration. It will always be more or less damp, and only things which can be left all the year round without deteriorating should be stored in it. The ideal fishing hut contains at least two rooms, one for storing rough gear, such as ropes, grapnels, stakes, wire netting, cement, spade and bucket, billhook, axe, saw, crowbars and sledge-hammer, boat oars, rullocks, and anchors; the other for storing a certain amount of fishing tackle, and for use as a haven, in which the fisherman and his guests can, if necessary, have a meal and make themselves warm.

This second room will be warmer and more comfortable if it is matchboarded inside. It should contain a table and benches, an iron stove and plenty of fuel, a kettle, tea and sugar in tins, and, perhaps, a Primus, so that a hot drink can be brewed while the other stove gets going. Another useful provision, from the human point of view, is a first-aid outfit against a possible hook - wound, viper - bite, sprained ankle, or broken leg.

The best safeguard against the ill effects of falling into a river is a bottle of whisky, and it will keep indefinitely in the hut, which beer will not. There should be pegs for wet coats, waders, and fishing bags, long shelves for rods, and two or three line driers fixed to the wall; cupboards, also, should be fitted, which can contain bottles of natural baits, spare rod rings, twine, thread, wax, adhesive tape, hammer and nails, a heavy pair of pliers, and a bottle of oil. Gaffs, tailers, and nets can be left in the hut, but not rods, flies, lines, spring balances, or any other tackle, unless the hut is frequently visited and aired. If a permanent weighing machine is wanted, have a bar-and-weight arrangement, which the damp will not affect. Another useful fitting for the hut is a maximum-and-minimum thermometer, which should be hung permanently outside, and will provide valuable information for each day's fishing.

For the improvement of the river as a whole the

owners must act together, and when they do so they can legally exercise far greater powers than they can when acting individually. The Salmon and Freshwater Fisheries Act, 1923, provides for the constitution of a Fishery Board, to control the fishing in any specific area, upon application to the Minister of Agriculture and Fisheries. The application may be made by any existing Fishery Board, by the County Council, by the owners of a quarter of the fisheries to be controlled, or by any association of persons who are, in the Minister's opinion, sufficiently representative of fishing interests within the area. The members of the Board include those appointed by the County Council, and those representing the netsmen and any licenced rod fishermen for fish other than salmon. They also include all owners or occupiers of fisheries rated at upwards of £30 a year, and everyone who owns land of the value of £100 a year and upwards, which fronts for a mile or more upon water in the area containing salmon, trout, or other fish, and who have the right to fish in such water, and who pay licence duty.

The powers which the Board can exercise under the Act are very wide indeed, and cover pretty well all the activities necessary for keeping a fishery in good order. They can grant licences to fish, and prosecute anyone who fishes without one; they can appoint water-bailiffs with powers of search; they can also alter the close season, so long as it remains not less than ninety-two days, and can impose suitable interregnums on the activities of netsmen. They can also conduct hatchery experiments, stop pollution, and build fish passes.

Several large-scale experiments, notably one at Cultus Lake, British Columbia, which lasted during the years 1930 to 1934, have shown it to be very doubtful whether the institution of salmon hatcheries is worth while. It is true that the mortality between the egg and the parr stage can be reduced by modern hatchery methods from about 97 per cent to about 25 per cent. But the Cultus Lake experiments showed that the mortality of the young fish *after* they reach the sea is about 90 per cent. It also showed that if the fish are left to themselves, there is still, in spite of the terrific mortality, an adequate balance in favour of the increase of the fish, *i.e.* from the 4500 eggs produced by the average pair of spawning fish, about eleven adults return to the river—enough to make a large fishing drain possible without damaging the stock.

Pollution is a highly technical subject, about which many books have been written. The Thames, the Tyne, and the Clyde are perhaps the most notable instances of fine salmon rivers which have been ruined by pollution. The questions usually resolve themselves into a war between the industrial interest and the fishing interest, and whichever is most valuable will probably win. But it should be noted in this connection that domestic sewage is often just as dangerous as industrial effluents.

Fish passes, on the other hand, do nothing but good to everyone—even, in the long run, to the people who have to pay for them! The most pressing need for fish passes is seen in the Canadian rivers, scores of which have been completely ruined, as far as salmon fishing goes, by indiscriminate building of dams for electric power. The cost of a high pass is of course very great, but the value of the improvement of the salmon fisheries —not so much in fish caught, but in traffic for the railways and the countryside in general—would, in most cases, well repay the initial outlay.

The construction of a fish pass, is, like the treatment of pollution, a highly technical subject, which is rather outside the scope of a book on fishing. The most important characteristics of a fish pass may however be mentioned. The most usual form is a "ladder" of open boxes, made usually by blasting a series of deep hollows in the rock at one side of the dam, and walling them with concrete in such a way that the water overflows with a small fall from one into the next. This has been found to be the most successful form, for it provides an ample amount of quiet water for the fish to rest in, and by rounding the lips of the boxes the amount of "white", or aerated, water in the pass can be reduced to a minimum. Where the amount of compensation water—the water that can be allowed to flow through the pass—is limited, the lips of the boxes should be made with a dip in the centre, so that even if the quantity of water is diminished, there will always be sufficient depth for the salmon to ascend in comfortably. The outflow should, if possible, be placed in deep water in a part of the pool where the fish are likely to notice it and use it, and the inflow must correspondingly be placed where the descending kelts and smolts can find it, although, if there is plenty of water beneath the main fall into which the descending fish can tumble without hurting themselves, the position of the inflow of the pass is not so important. The box-ladder type of fish pass has been found to answer best, although scores of designs have been tried out. Lamond in *The Gentle Art* tells a nice story of a fisherman who is reputed to have described to some spinner of tall yarns the trial of a new kind of salmon ladder. It was an arrangement of buckets on an endless chain working over a couple of pulleys, which had been placed against the face of the fall, so that the weight of water pressing on the descending buckets would bring up the full ones, containing, of course, the ascending salmon. Fish were seen to go up in the ascending buckets, but none of them were ever seen to go on above the fall. The mystery was solved when an old cock salmon was caught in the pool below, with a large bag of worms tied round his middle, and it was realised that he had been charging the others a worm a turn for a trip on the merry-go-round!

APPENDIX

A SALMON FISHERMAN'S TABLES

For finding the weight of a fish from measurements alone a formula is better than a scale, because by taking into account the girth measurement it allows automatically for the condition of the fish. An accurate formula for finding the weight of a fish from measurements alone is that given by Hewitt in *Secrets of the Salmon*:

$$\frac{\text{Girth}^2 \text{ in inches} \times \text{Length in inches}}{800} = \text{Weight of the fish in lb.}$$

There is still much confusion of hook scales. Many of the local scales, such as the Kendal, the Carlisle, and the Dublin, have largely dropped out of use; but there are still the Redditch scale, the Pennell, or "New", scale, and recently a further scale has been put forward which is called the Rational scale and is based on the length of the hook from the bend to the neck, *i.e.* the base of the eye.

The Pennell scale has nothing to recommend it. The old traditional Redditch scale is based on the gauge of the wire of which the hooks are made, and, being more generally used than any other, it is the scale which it is safest to quote when asking for flies. It is a pity that some scale having a more direct relation to the size of the hook itself—either to the width of the gape or to the length of the shank—should not be adopted. But the change would mean great expense to the makers. In the meantime, the Redditch scale is the one that is most used.

The following is a comparative list of the Pennell and Redditch sizes:

Redditch scale: 6/0, 5/0, 4/0, 3/0, 2/0, 1/0, 1, 2, 3, 4, 5, 6,
Pennell scale: 20, 19, 18, 17, 16, 15 14, 13, 12, 11, 10, 9,

Redditch scale: 7, 8, 9, 10, 11, 12, 13, 14, 15, 16, 17,   18.
Pennell scale: 8, 7, 6, 5, 4, 3, 2, 1, 0, 00, 000, 0000.

GUT SIZES AND BREAKING STRAINS

MONOFILAMENT NYLON				SILKWORM GUT		
Metric Diameter, Mm.	Breaking Strain, Kilos.	Diameter, Inches	Breaking Strain, lb.	British Standard Wire Gauge	Old Gut Notation	Silkworm Gut Breaking Strain, lb.
·14	0·9	·0055	2	39	6X Drawn	⎫
·16	1·1	·0063	2½	38	5X ,,	1½ to 2½
·18	1·7	·0071	3¾	37	4X ,,	⎭
·20	1·8	·0078	4	36	3X ,,	⎫
·22	2·4	·0086	5¼	35	2X ,,	2½ to 3½
·24	2·8	·0094	6¼	34	1X ,,	⎭
·26	3·0	·0102	7	33	0X ,,	⎫
·28	3·6	·0110	8	31	½ ,,	2¾ to 4½
·30	4·3	·0118	9½	30	¼ ,,	⎭
·35	5·6	·0138	12¼	28	8/5 Regular	3½ to 5
·40	7·5	·0157	16½	27	6/5 Padron	6½ to 7
·45	9·4	·0177	20¾	26	4/5 Marana	7 to 8
·50	11·6	·0197	25½	25	2/5 Royal Hebra	⎫
·55	13·6	·0216	30	..	1/5 Crown	8 to 10
·60	16·8	·0236	37	24	0/5 ,,	⎭

FLY LINE SIZES

Letters	Diameter, Mm.	Diameter, Inches	Letters	Diameter, Mm.	Diameter, Inches
AAA	1·778	·070	E	1·016	·040
AA	1·651	·065	F	0·889	·035
A	1·524	·060	G	0·762	·030
B	1·397	·055	H	0·635	·025
C	1·270	·050	I	0·559	·022
D	1·143	·045			

Taper is denoted by the appropriate succession of letters, *e.g.* a heavy double-tapered line might be lettered GAAG, indicating a thickness of ·030″ at each point and ·065″ at the centre.

(AFTM numbers, applied to lines, do not refer to size, but to the weight of the outer 30 feet, whatever the size or type.)

218

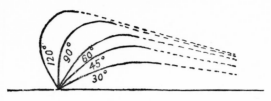

ROD TABLE

(Showing the approximate maximum pull at the tip of the rod that can be exerted when the butt is at various angles to the horizontal, without danger of breaking or damaging the rod.)

Rod	Length	Weight	Pull at Tip in lb. at Various Angles of Butt				
			120°	90°	60°	45°	30°
Fly rod .	16 ft.	33 oz.	1·5	2·0	3·25	4·5	8·25
Fly rod .	14 ft.	18 oz.	1·25	1·75	2·0	3·0	4·75
Fly rod .	12 ft.	14 oz.	1·0	1·25	2·25	4·0	7·0
Fly rod .	12 ft.	12 oz.	0·75	1·0	2·0	4·0	7·0
Fly rod .	10 ft. 6 ins.	7 oz.	0·5	0·75	1·25	2·0	3·0
Spinning rod	10 ft.	17 oz.	2·0	2·25	4·0	6·0	9·5
Spinning rod	9 ft.	6 oz.	0·75	1·0	1·5	2·0	3·0

INDEX

Aaro, River, 5
Action of a fly rod, 63, 122
Adhesive tape, 29
Adipose fin, 204
Aerial reel, 160, 167
Aerial tackle, 172
"AFTM" Standards for rods and
    lines, 63, 123, 218
Air Cel line, 123
Alevin, 204
Algae, 207
Altex reel, 162, 166, 173
Ambassadeur reel, 161
American fishing, 55, 56, 117, 120,
    140, 142-144, 146, 151, 164
Anti-fly dope and clothing, 32, 33
Anti-kink leads, 155, 156, 166
    plate, 156, 157, 172
April run, 8
Armathwaite, 40-41
Artificial spate, 211

Backing, 61, 62, 124
Bag, fishing, 31
Bag, record, 5
Bags, previous, importance of
    knowing, 9
Baggot, 206
Bait, depth at which to fish, 18
    illumination of, 19
    kind of, 14, 16-18
    path of, 18, 19
    size of, 2, 17, 18, 148, 166, 173
    weight of, 148, 168
    wooden plug, 18, 151, 152
Bait-casting, with revolving-drum
    reel, 166-168
    with stationary-drum reel, 173,
    174
Baiting with worms, 192, 193
Baits, artificial, 149, 151, 152
    mounting, 153-155, 168, 183, 184
    natural, 149, 150, 152
Baking salmon, 112
Balaclava helmet, 32
Balance, spring, 31
    in tackle, 118, 121, 122

Balfour-Kinnear, D., 41, 122, 138
Banks, repairing, 211
Barbed wire in river-bed, 41
Barnes, Dr Stanley, 50
Basses for packing salmon, 109
Bayonet tackle, 183, 184
Beaching a salmon, 105
Bearings, taking, in a lake, 200,
    201
Beat, distance of, from sea, 7
    improving a particular, 211, 212
    near the sea, 8
Beats, good and bad, 8
Beauly Snow Fly, 47, 87
Begg, Dr, 137
Bleeding a salmon, 107, 109
Blind-cord, 30, 107
Blood knot, 50-52
Blood loop, 53
Blowline, 141, 197
"Blueshank", 119
Boat, disturbing salmon, 37
    fishing from a, 89, 90, 197-199
Boatman, 89, 90, 196, 197
Boil made by current over a rock,
    12, 87, 92
Boiling salmon, 111, 112
Bottling salmon, 112, 113
Boulder-lies, artificial, 208, 209
    natural, 12, 87, 129, 196
Box, fly, 48, 49
    rod, 33-34
Braking of a spinning reel, 163,
    167, 168, 173, 175, 176
Bridge rings, 66, 121
British Columbia, 213, 214
British Standard Wire Gauge, 49
Brogues, 24-26
Bull trout, 206
Buttons, rod, 122

Cairnton, 114, 115, 159
    knot, 54, 55, 87, 159
Camp shedding, 211
Canadian fishing, 8, 32, 117, 123,
    143, 146
Cane gaff handle, 26

16

Caprice, 17
Carbonic acid gas for preserving
   prawns, 181
Carborundum, 29, 30
Careless fishing, 2, 35, 123
Carrying salmon, 107
Cast, altering angle of, 94
   angle of, 91, 94
   back-handed, 73
   gut, for greased-line fishing,
      117, 120, 121
   length of, 55, 56, 117, 118,
      145
      object of, 49
      tapered, 56
      tying, 50-53
   overhead, 70-73, 75, 77
   Spey, 73-75, 92
   square, 78, 79, 85
   switch, 73-75, 92
   upstream, 94, 145, 174, 175
Casting a worm, 191
Casting, "aids" to, 79, 80, 83-85, 93
   down to a fish, 95
   from a boat, 197, 198
   from which bank?, 18-20
   practice, 69, 70, 166-168
   radially, 130
   with a mend in the line, 77, 92,
      131
   with a revolving-drum spinning
      reel, 166-168
   with a stationary-drum spinning
      reel, 173, 174
Cast-maker's loop knot, 53
Castle Connell rods, 63, 75, 138,
   165
Celluloid anti-kink plate, 157
Celluloid "leads", 156
Cerolene, 128
Chafe in spinning, 158
Chaytor, A. H., 43, 50, 109, 127,
   142
Checks, reel, 67, 68
Clay patches in river-bed, 41
Clear water, 18
Clothing, anti-fly, 32
   warm, 36
   waterproof, 23-26
Clyde, River, 214
Cock salmon, 202, 203
Cobra reel, 68
Cold water, 18, 114
Colour of water, 118

Coming short, 83
Compensation water, 215
Cooking salmon, 111-113
Copper wire for mounting baits,
   154
Corkscrew, 30
County Council, 213
Crosfield, Ernest, 117, 127, 137,
   140
Crossing fast water, 39
Croy, 130, 209, 210
Cultus Lake experiment, 213,
   214
Curd in a salmon, 108, 109
Curled line, throwing a, 77, 143,
   145
Current, effect of, on fly and line,
   76, 78, 79, 82-85, 115
Currents, surface, indicating sal-
   mon's position, 10

Dalmatia, 3
Damp, 49, 212
Dangers in salmon fishing, 3, 36-
   44
"Dangle", fly at the, 83, 93, 97,
   133
Dapping, 141, 191
Dartmoor, 179
Dead reckoning, 7
Dee, River, 8, 114, 115, 127
Deep wading, 37-40
Deer fat, 128
Deerstalker, 26
Depth, affecting size of bait, 18
   at which to fish, 18, 21, 30
Depth, at which salmon lie, 9, 14
   noting, 200
Detergent for sinking cast, 128
Devons, 151
Digestive powers of salmon, 15
Diocletian, 3
Disgorging, 15
Disturbing salmon, 36, 37
Dope, anti-fly, 32
Double Dart, River, 4, 35
Double-tapered line, 59-61, 63
Downstream method of sunk-fly
   fishing, 81-86
Drag, 77-80, 82-84, 92, 126-128,
   131, 133, 145
Dropper, 137, 138, 140, 141
Drought, 8, 14, 135
Dry flies, 142-144

INDEX

Drying flights, 169
lines, 33, 62
waders, 44
"Dub" of a pool, 6, 11, 12, 21
Dyeing sprats, 149
Dynamite, 210

"Early" river, 7, 8
"Ease", finding an, 10
"Eases", types of, 11-13, 92
Eating salmon, 108, 111-113
Echo-sounder, viii
Eden, River, 4, 40, 41
Edwards, Alan, 41
Eel-tail bait, 149, 150
Eggs, salmon's, 203, 204, 214
Elastic bands for mounting baits, 155
Erosion, 209

Faeroe Islands, 36
Fall, as an obstacle to salmon, 210
Fall of a river, rate of, 11
Fascines, 211
Fear in salmon, 2
Feeding, of salmon in fresh water, 9, 14, 15
stations, 10
teeth, 202
Felt, compressed, for brogue soles, 25
Ferrule for gaff handle, 26
Ferrules, rod, 65, 66
Field, the, 43
Findhorn, River, 4
Fineness in tackle, 2, 127, 177
Finland, 32
Fins, celluloid, for flights, 153
First-aid outfit, 212
Fish-carrier, 30, 107
Fish passes, 210, 214, 215
Fishermen's dead reckoning, 7
knot, 52
Fishery Boards, 204, 213
Fishing a pool, 87-95
fine, 21, 177
commercial, vii, viii
cost of, vi
as a holiday industry, vi-viii
hut, 211, 212
rod, as a social necessity, vi-ix, xii
without local knowledge, 12

16 *a*

"Fixed-drum", 162
Flask, 31
Flax, backing, 61
line, 141
Flies, dressings of, 119, 124-125, 144
dry, 142-144
drying, 49
for greased-line fishing, 118-120, 124, 125
home-tied, 47
weight of, 46, 59, 97
Flights, 152-154, 166, 169, 170, 182-184
Float fishing, 189
Flood, effect on lies, 14
Fly, as food, 15, 16
boxes, 48, 49
changing, 93
control, 76-80, 116, 117
depth of, 18
drawn upstream, 95
fishing—16-18; and spinning compared, 148
freeing from a snag or tree, 89, 90, 91
kind of, 16, 46, 87, 124, 125
position of, 83, 85, 86, 97, 115
rod—see Rod, fly
size of, 2, 21, 45, 46, 58, 59, 86, 93, 120, 135
skidding, 97
skimming, 136-140
sunk, 45-68
working the, 81, 88, 97, 127, 128, 133, 134
Flyer, on stationary-drum reels, 162, 163, 173
Flying Salmon, 41
Fog, 20
Formalin, 150, 181
Forty-pounders, 5
Foxford, ix
Frail, carpenter's, 107, 109, 110
Fraser, Major R. J., 142
Fresh-run salmon, 105, 106
Friction in spinning, 162, 164
Frying salmon, 112
Fuller's earth, xii

Gaff, long-handled, 26, 198
pocket, 28, 29
sling for, 27, 28
telescopic, 27
Gaffing, 103-105

223

Gear, proportion in, 2, 45, 46
  storing, 33
Gentle Art, The, 215
Gillie, 106
Glare, 31, 125
Glass "leads", 156
"Glide", 11, 13, 14
Glitter, 21, 27, 49, 145
Gloaming, fishing in the, 129
Glycerine, 150
Golden dye, 149
Granite river-bed, 41
Grease, for greased-line, 128
  on the gut cast, 128
Greased line, 16, 84, 85, 114-134, 171
  compared with sunk-fly technique, 82-86, 115, 130, 131
  objects of, 116
  reasons for a, 115, 116, 126
  value of, 115, 116, 127
  when useful, 114, 115
Greenheart as a material for rods, 65, 165
Greenland, vii
Grilling salmon, 112
Grilse, 206
Grimersta, River, 5, 211
Grimsby fishermen, 36
Gut, silkworm, xi
  cracking and knuckling, 49, 56
  flash in, 21, 49, 121
  qualities of, 49
  scale, 49, 218
  sizes, 49, 50, 56, 57, 120, 145, 218
  soaking, 49
  strength of, 49, 218
  trade names of, 218
Gut-shyness, 21, 116-118, 136, 137

Haar, 20, 129
Hampshire, 142
Handlining, 101
Harling, 89, 90
Hatcheries, 213, 214
Hazel gaff handle, 26
Head-and-tailing, 145
Hebrides, 211
Height gauge for a lake, 200
Height of river, effect of—on change of outfit, 21; on kind of bait, 16; on lies, 14, 15; on size of bait, 17
  noting, 31

Hewitt, E. R., 120, 123, 138, 140, 217
Hewitt's formula for weighing salmon, 32, 217
Hexworthy, 179
Highland, pool, 6
  scenery, 4
Hook, barb of, 47, 48, 119, 170
  point of, 47, 48, 89, 93, 119
  scales, 30, 217
  size of, 46, 47
  weight of, 47
Hook-gut-and-line scale, 33
Hooked salmon, behaviour of, 5, 97
Hooking, safest place for, 83, 118
  salmon, 83, 97, 114, 118, 132, 133, 143, 152, 153, 170, 171, 174, 182
Hovers, 10
Hunger, 15
Hut, fishing, 211, 212
Hutton, Arthur, 31, 205

Ice, 8, 111
Iceland, 32
Illingworth type of reel, 162
Illumination of bait, 18-20
Incubation, 204
Inertia in spinning reels, 160-162
International Commission for the Northwest Atlantic Fisheries, viii
  Council for the Exploration of the Sea, viii
  waters, viii
Ireland, vii, ix, 141, 178, 197
Irfon, River, 13, 41
Irish Fisheries Trust, ix

Jardine lead, 156
Jaw, salmon's, 118, 120, 132, 133, 203
Jefferies, Richard, 108
Jock Scott, 47
Johnston, H. W., 205
July fishing, 20
Jumping salmon, 7, 99, 145

Keeping out of sight, 21, 146
Kelt, 29, 105, 106, 210, 215
Kendal Scale, 217
Killing salmon, 30
Knife, fisherman's, 30

INDEX

Knots, 50-55, 87
Knots in Nylon, 50
Knuckling of gut, 56

La Branche, G. M., 143
Laces for brogues, 26
Ladder, salmon, 210, 214, 215
Lakes, finding salmon in, 195, 196
Lamond, 215
Landing salmon, 102, 106
Lashing for gaff handle, 26
"Late" river, 7, 8
Lavender oil, 32
Lead, in spinning, 151, 155
  wire, 183-185, 193
Leader, gut, object of, 49
"Leading" the line, 85, 131
Leads, anti-kink, 155, 156, 166,
  173
"Leads", glass, 156
Lease, 7, 8, 17
Leather soles for brogues, 25
Leg waders, 23
Letters to a Salmon Fisher's Sons, 43,
  50, 109
Lice, 15
Licence to fish, 17, 213
Lies, artificial, 208-210
  of salmon, 10-13, 92, 93
Light, 18-21, 31
Line, Air Cel, 123
  double-tapered, 59, 60
  -drier, 33
  drying, 62
  floating, 115-118
  for lake fishing, 199
  for prawning, 187
  for worming, 191, 192
  freeing snagged, 100, 101
  giving slack, 97, 100
  level, 61, 159
  "mending", 79, 80, 83
  "shooting", 73, 75-78
  splicing, 61
  sunk, 47, 60
  tacky, 62
  tapered—purpose of, 58, 139;
    strength of, 61; weight of, 57-
    60, 123, 124, 148
  throwing a curved, 77
  throwing a slack, 76, 77, 132,
    145
Lines, AFTM Standards for, 63,
  218

Lines (*contd.*)
  classification of, 60, 63, 218
  plastic, xii, 1, 60-64
  spinning, 159, 160, 162, 163,
    166
Llangamarch, 13
Loach, 149, 150
Local knowledge, 10-12, 195, 196
Local methods, 2
Lomond, Loch, 197
Lonsdale Library, 181
Loop knots, 53
Loss of weight in salmon, 31
Low water, 17

Mackintosh jacket, 26
Maiden fish, 206
Malloch reel, 162
March, fishing, 20
  run, 8
Matches, 31
Mauranger Fjord, 190
Maxillary bones, 204
Maxwell, Sir Herbert, 137
May-fly, 142-144, 197
Measuring salmon, 31, 32
Medway, River, 10
"Mend", using wind to create,
  131
"Mending", 79, 80, 83, 88, 92,
  115, 130, 131
  downstream, 134
Midges, 32, 33
Migration, 7
Minister of Agriculture and Fish-
  eries, 213
Minnows, 149, 150, 172
Mist, 20
Mortality among salmon, 204, 205,
  207, 214
Moy, River, ix

Nails for brogues, 25
Naylor, Mr, 5
Net, 104
Netsmen, 210, 213
Netting, vii
  offshore, vii, viii
Nettles as packing for salmon, 110
New Scale, 217
Nobbs, Percy, 10, 32
Norway, 32, 190, 191
Norwegian record salmon, 5
Norwegian run, 8

225

Notebook, 31
Notes to make when salmon-
  fishing, 31, 106, 199
Nylon, xi, xii
  advantages of, 49
  designation, 49
  knots for, 50-55
  sizes and breaking strains, 218
  slipperiness of, 50
  strength of, 120, 218
  for spinning, 159, 160, 172
  taper in casts, 56

Obstacles to salmon's progress up
  river, 9
October run, 8
Oil of lavender, 32
Oil of white birch, 32
Oiling tackle, 33
Old-fashioned tackle, 2
Orthodox technique compared
  with greased-line technique,
  82-86, 115
Outcrop of rock, 12
Outfit, change of, 21, 123, 124,
  148
Overhand loop knot, 53
Overhead cast, 70-73, 75-78
Overrunning, 160, 167, 173
Oxygen, 12, 14, 135

Packing salmon, 109, 111
Pain, salmon's insensitiveness to,
  30, 97
Painting gaff handle, 37
Palmer dry-fly dressing, 143, 144
Paper clips, 30, 86, 89
Parr, 117, 204-205
Patching waders, 44
Path of bait, 18-20
Pattern of fly, 46, 47, 119, 120,
  124, 125
Pennell Scale, 217
  tackle, 193
Pflueger reel, 161, 164, 168
Phantoms, 151
Piano wire, 157
Pigskin cast case, 30
Pipe, 32
Plastic lines, 1, 60-64
Playing salmon, 96-103, 176, 198
Pleasure of salmon fishing, 3
Plug baits, 18, 151, 152
Poaching, vii, 210

Point of hook, 47, 48, 89, 93, 119
Pollution, vii, 214
Pool, anatomy of a, 6, 11, 12
  fishing a, 87, 88, 91
  Highland, 6
  light in a, 18
  normal type of, 11
  whereabouts of salmon in a, 9
Position of salmon, in a pool, 9, 10,
  14, 129, 135, 145
  in lakes, 195, 196
"Pots", 12
Powers of Fishery Board, 213
Prawn, as bait, 16, 17
  as food for salmon, 15, 16
  as spinning bait, 149, 150, 154,
  173, 181
  frightening salmon, 180
  mounting, 183, 184
  scaring salmon, 17, 24
  tackle, 154, 182-184
Prawning, 16
Preserving prawns, 150, 181, 182
Priest, 30, 106
Proportion in tackle, 2, 45, 46, 56,
  60, 117, 118, 139, 148, 159
"Pulling off", 93, 97, 136, 146
"Pulling through", 140
Pumping fish in, 124, 176
Purple King, 47
Python reel, 68

Radial casting, 130
Rain, advances run, 8
Rate of fall of a river, 11
Rational Scale, 217
Record bag, 5
  salmon, 5
Redd, 203, 204
Redditch Scale, 217
"Redshank", 119
Reed, River, 137
Reedsmouth, 137
Reel fittings, variable, 67, 165
Reels, fixed-spool, xii (see also
  Reels, stationary-drum)
  fly, 67, 68
  multiplying, 124, 161
  oil for, 33
  revolving-drum, 160-164, 166,
  169, 172
  spinning, 160-163;—braking,
  68, 163, 167, 168, 173, 175,
  176

Reels *(contd.)*
stationary-drum, 160-163, 172, 173, 176, 191
Restrictions in lease, 17
Righyni, R. V., 125
Rings, 66, 121
Rising water, danger of, when wading, 40
River, beats, good and bad, 8
bed, types of, 40, 41
danger of sudden rise in, 40
"early", 7, 8
distance of, from sea, 7
River, height of, effect of—on kind of bait, 16; on lies, 14; on size of bait, 18
"late", 7, 8
rate of fall of, 11
Rock, "boil", 12, 13, 88, 93
faults, 12
outcrop, 12, 88
Rod box, 33, 34
buttons, 26, 67, 122
change of, 21
for prawning, 187
for worming, 191
fly, action of, 63
choosing, 45, 46, 62, 63, 65
double-handed, 65
fibreglass, xi, 65
fittings for, 66, 67
greenheart, 65
length of, 1, 63-65, 121, 124
power-factor for, 62, 63, 218
pull of, 2, 58, 124, 219
purpose of, 45, 46, 57, 58
split-bamboo, xi, 65
strength of, 2, 58, 59, 63, 65
weight of, 65, 124, 219
proper angle of, whilst playing a fish, 99, 120, 124, 169, 176, 218
pull of, 2, 58
rings, 66, 121
Rod table, 218
Rods, Castle Connell, 63, 75
for dry-fly fishing, 145
for greased-line fishing, 121-123
for surface fishing, 139
number of, 123
spinning, 148, 149, 164-166, 172
stowing, 33
Rolex reel, 161
Rough water, 11, 37

Rubber, brogues, 24, 25
ferrule for gaff handle, 26
rod-buttons, 26, 67, 122
Run, duration of the, 8
influences affecting, 8
when occurs, 8

Salmon and Freshwater Fisheries Act, 1923, 101, 102, 110, 213
Salmon and Sea Trout, 137
Salmon, apathetic, 18, 82, 127
as food, 108, 111, 113
behaviour of, hooked, 5
in fresh water, 15, 149
bleeding, 107
bored, 17
caprice in, 17
carrying, 107
changes in, whilst in fresh water, 202, 203
clean-run, 105, 106
conservation of, vi-ix, xii, 207-216
dazzled by sun, 19
digestive powers, 15
feeding in fresh waters, 9, 14-16, 149
fishing, dangers in, 3, 36, 37-44; pleasures of, 3
food of, 205
frightened by prawn, 180
influences affecting run of, 8
jumping, 7
loss of weight in—after capture, 31; whilst in fresh water, 31
nomenclature of, 204-206
position of, behind a rock, 12
preoccupation of, in fresh water, 9, 14-16
record, 5
running through, 7, 14
scarcity of, vi-ix, xii
scared, 17, 36, 94
shyness in, 2, 4, 17, 21, 36, 116, 136, 137
sight of, 21, 129
stirring up, 5, 36, 37, 101, 138, 146
stopping a, 100
stopping in a pool, 12
study of the, 4
sulking, 101
taking a fly, 96
when present in river, 7

Salmon (*contd.*)
whereabouts of, in each pool,
9, 10, 12, 135
Salmon Tactics, 10, 32
Salmon Taking Times, 125
Salmon's tail, knuckle of, 105
Salt and water, as a preserving
medium, 150
Sandstone bed, 40
Scale-reading, 205
Scales, hook, 30, 217
Scenery, Highland, 4
Scenery, Lowland, 4
*Science of Spinning for Salmon and
Trout*, 181
Scissors, 29, 30
Scotch mist, 20
Scotland, vi, vii, 32, 177
Sea, distance of beat from, 7
salmon in, vii, viii, 205
Secrets of the Salmon, 140, 217
September run, 8
Shale outcrop, 41
Shallow water, 18
Shank of hook, 54, 119
Shannon, River, 81
Sharpening hooks, 47, 48
Sheet bend, 55, 87
Shingle, bank, 12, 38, 41
beaching a salmon on, 60
Shooting line, 73, 75-78, 88
Shyness in salmon, 2, 4, 17, 36,
116, 136, 137
Sight, keeping out of, 21, 146
of salmon, 21
Silex reel, 160, 167
Silk spinning lines, 159, 160, 163,
166
Silver Doctor, 47
Simplex leads, 184, 193
Size of bait, 2, 17, 31, 148, 166,
173
of fly, 2, 17, 21, 31, 45, 46, 58,
59, 86, 93, 118-120, 135
of gut, 50, 57, 218
of hook, 46, 47
of water, 118, 176, 177
Skidding fly, 97
Skimming fly, 136-140
Slabs in river-bed, 41
Slack line, throwing a, 76, 77,
132, 145
Slip knot, 54
Smell, salmon's sense of, 181

Smoking salmon, 113
Smolts, 205, 210, 215
Snag, 89, 100, 101, 211
Snake rings, 66
Snow, 8, 111
Socks, wading, 36, 41
Sou'wester, 26
Spare gear, 21, 22
Spate, artificial, 211
Spawning, 202-206
grounds, 9, 11
Spey cast, 73-75, 92
Spiling, 210, 211
Spinning and fly-fishing compared,
148, 159
Spinning bait, depth of, 18
effect of, in scaring salmon, 2,
17
heavy, outfit for, 166
in lakes, 197, 198
light, outfit for, 172, 173
lines, 158-160, 162, 163, 166
reels, 160-163; brakes for, 68
tactics, 169-171
traces, 157-159
Splicing lines, 61
Split-bamboo fly rods, 65
Split shot, 184, 193
Sportsmanship, 190, 191
Sprats, 149, 166
Spring, fishing, 20, 87, 88
run, 8, 14
Spring balance, 8, 14
Square cast in spinning, 170
Staff, wading, 21, 38, 39
Stances for casting, 211
Stationary-drum reel, 160-163,
166, 172, 173, 176, 191
Stewart tackle, 193
"Stickle", 12, 129, 194
Sticky tape, 29
Stiletto, 30
St. John, vi
Stock of salmon, 214
Stockings, wading, 36
Stomach, salmon's, 15
Stones, throwing, 101, 102
Stopping a salmon, 100
Storing tackle, 33
waders, 44
Strength, of outfit, 46
of rod, 59, 60, 63, 65
Striking, 83, 97, 118, 119, 132,
146, 147, 185, 186, 194

"Striking tension", 173
"Stripping in" line, 140
Sugar and water as a preserving medium, 150
"Summer fish", 206
Summer, fishing, 20
run, 8
Sun, position of, 18-20
Sundal, 190
Sunk fly, 45-68
how modified by greased-line technique, 82-86
method, traditional, 81-83, 85
purpose of, 82
Surface, fishing, 18, 116-118, 135-147
fly, methods of fishing, 136
indications of salmon's position, 10
Surface spinners, 151, 152
"Surges", 6, 11, 12, 40, 130
Swimming in waders, 42-44
Switch cast, 73-75, 92
Swivels, 33, 154, 155, 158, 159, 166, 172, 184, 193

Tackle, improvements in, v
old-fashioned, 1
proportion in, 2, 45, 46
releaser, 30, 89, 91, 92
spare, 21, 22
storing, 33
Tackles, worming, 192, 193
Tacky lines, remedy for, 62
Tail of a pool, 6, 11, 12, 21
Tailer, 26, 29, 105
Tailing by hand, 105
Take-off below a weir, 210
"Taking" places, 10
Tamar, River, 4
Tape, adhesive, 29
Tape measure, 31
Tapered casts, 56
Tarporeno, 151, 152
Taverner, Eric, 181
Tavy, River, viii
Tchernavin, Dr, 203
Teeth of salmon, 202, 203
Teign, River, 5
Temperature, 7, 14, 18, 20, 21, 31, 82, 114, 116, 128, 142, 144, 199
Terraces in river-bed, 40
Test, River, 142

Thames, River, 214
Thermometer, 30, 129, 212
Thick water, 17, 37, 38
Thomas, Terry, 125
Thread line, 16, 172-177, 192
"Throat" of a pool, 11, 12, 14, 21
Time, of day, 20, 31
of year, 7, 14, 16, 20, 31, 142
spent by salmon in river and sea, 204, 206
Timing a cast, 72
with a revolving-drum reel, 167, 168
"Tinning" salmon, 112
Tobacco, 31, 32
Trace, for prawning, 184
for worming, 193
Traces, spinning, 157-159, 172
"Traveller", 89, 102
Tree, freeing fly from a, 89, 91, 92
Trevethin, Lord, 35
Triangles, essential qualities of, 153
Trolling, 197, 198
"Trotting" a prawn, 187
Trout, 6, 204
compared with parr, 204
Trout fisherman's viewpoint, 10, 15, 21, 23
Trout rod, 145, 172
Turle knot, 55, 87, 159, 193
Tweed, River, 5
Twine, 29, 89, 92, 107
Tying gut, 50-55
and wire to swivels, 159
Tyne, River, 137, 138, 142, 214

Ugie, River, 128
Umbilical sac, 204
Underhand cast, 73, 75, 77, 78
Universal reel fittings, 67
Upstream cast, 94, 174
Uptrace spinners, 155

Waders, fit of, 23, 24
leg, 23
patching, 44
storing, 44
swimming in, 42-44
trouser, 23, 24, 26, 35
Wading, 27, 35-44, 88, 94
disturbance caused by, 36, 140
objects of, 36
socks, 25, 31
staff, 21, 38, 39

Wading (*contd.*)
  stockings, 36
  sudden rise of river whilst, 43, 44
  warmth whilst, 42
  whilst wearing a belt, 43, 44
  without waders, 35, 36
Waggling the rod, 81, 88
Waist, 87, 92
Walking fish in, 102, 177
Watch spring, for rod repairs, 29
Water, clear, 18, 117, 120, 148
  cold, 18
  colour and size of, 118
  deep, 18
  height of—affecting change of outfit, 21; affecting kind of bait, 16; affecting lies, 14; affecting size of bait, 18, 148
  low, 17, 116, 117
  quiet, 11, 37
  rough, 11, 37
  shallow, 18
  spoiling the, 17
  streamy, 129, 135, 140
  strong, 38, 39
  temperature of, 18, 20
  thick, 17, 18, 37
  warm, 18
Watermanship, 126
Waterproofs, 26
Waxed twine, 29
Weather, bright, 87, 116, 117
  cold, 114
  effect of, on stock of fish, 8
  hot, 135, 142-144

Weighing of salmon, 31
Weight, of gear, 31, 58
  of bait, 148
  of flies, 46
  of line, 57, 58
  loss of, in salmon, 31
  of wire in hooks, 47, 132
Whaleback, 38, 130
Whereabouts of salmon in each pool, 9, 10, 14
Whip finish, 27
Whisky in your boots, 42
Wild Sports of the Highlands, vi
Wilkinson, 47
Wind, effect of, on bait-casting, 168
  making use of, in casting, 131, 141
Wire, copper, for mounting baits, 154, 183, 184
  for spinning traces, 29, 157-159
  oil for, 33
"Wobblers", 151, 152
Wood, A. H. E., 79, 80, 84, 114-117, 122, 126
Wooden "plug" baits, 18, 151, 152
Working the fly, 81, 88, 97, 127, 128, 133, 134
Worming, 16, 17
Worms, as bait, 17
  as food for salmon, 15, 16
Wye, River, viii

Yarmouth Stores, 36

THE END